ROCK & ROLL HOTELS

SEX. DRUGS. FLUFFY PILLOWS.

ROCK & ROLL HOTELS

SEX. DRUGS. FLUFFY PILLOWS.

GREG SIMMONS

Rock 'n' Roll Hotels
Published in the United Kingdom in 2011 by
Punk Publishing Ltd
3 The Yard
Pegasus Place
London
SE11 5SD

www.punkpublishing.co.uk

A catalogue record of this book is available from the British Library.

ISBN: 978-1-906889-09-8
10 9 8 7 6 5 4 3 2 1

Printed and bound in Italy by Grafica Veneta

'When I check into a hotel I have them give me a call at 7a.m. so I can go to bed.'

Joe Walsh

CONTENTS

INTRODUCTION

'Keith', said Cy, a Londoner who had managed to retain his accent despite living in LA for 25 years, 'had a comeback capability which allowed him to… ' Cy's voice trailed off as he struggled to find the words that would succinctly sum up his old friend's inherent charm. My pen hovered expectantly over the last bit of space in a notebook already crammed with tales from those who inhabited other rock 'n' roll strata. Still, I had good reason to be poised in anticipation of hearing more about the myth-making rock deities. My raconteur, after all, was Cy Langston – The Who's first road manager. The 'Keith' in question was, as you've probably guessed, Keith Moon – loveable rogue and whirlwind drummer for the British band.

Despite my having already travelled to places as wide and varied as Amsterdam, New York and London – all in the name of research – the good folk at Punk Publishing saw fit to send me on a Hollywood hotel-crawl in order to fully validate my rock 'n' roll credentials. So, taking a cue from the Doors' lyrics inscribed on my hotel window ('Come on baby light my fire/Set the night on fire'), I intended to do just that and go out and schmooze with the rock-star contingent.

And, it is my intention that by diving in and discovering more about *Rock 'n' Roll Hotels* you, too, will sup heartily from rock 'n' roll's excess.

Ostensibly a travel guide for the diehard music fan, this book chronicles the steamy, the sexy and the downright scandalous antics that have helped place rock stars on the pedestal of egregious cool. For as our heroes and heroines blazed a trail across the globe, the triumvirate of 'sex, drugs and rock 'n' roll' invariably found a home in many a hotel where, behind the 'Do Not Disturb' hangers, proclivities for destruction, debauchery and defenestration could be exhausted. And it is precisely this that defines which hotels make it into the exclusive ranks of *Rock 'n' Roll Hotels* – wherever a troubadour drops his hat to let the party begin or, conversely, wherever stars close themselves off behind hotel doors to be alone and indulge in guilty pleasures.

So, you'll find that the hotels run the gamut of accommodation standards – from glittery five-star splendour (see George V, page 111) to unprepossessing motels fading into history (see Highland Gardens, page 49). Some hotels may break the bank, but not every rock 'n' roll hotel requires a rock-star's wallet; it's not about the cash, it's about the cachet. So, whether you'd like to glimpse rock-star living in a suite with its own bowling alley (see Hard Rock Las Vegas, page 65) or soak up the musky atmosphere of a long-ago era where a rock star, buffeted by booze and drugs, breathed their last (see The Joshua Tree Inn, page 61), it's down to you.

But this book also factors in a third type of hotel – one that caters to the needs of the touring musician. These hotels provide guitar and amplification servicing (see Sanctum Soho, page 139) staff who will take on the role of roadies (see BackStage Hotel, page 147) and, if you're a musician of some repute, there are those with 'paparazzi diversion' services (see Sunset Marquis, page 53).

Whichever type of hotel you choose to check into, just remember to check out. For all the glamorisation of rock 'n' roll living there are, inevitably, casualties. To that end, this book also offers a few cautionary tales. As Cy said, you need that 'comeback capability'. This can be hard to attain; even Moonie struggled to hold on to it in the end.

Here's to rock 'n' roll…
Greg Simmons

NORTH AMERICA

FAIRMONT THE QUEEN ELIZABETH

Two dozen roses – half of them red, half white – are left at the door of Suite 1742 every year on the anniversary of John Lennon's death: 8 December. This act of veneration is carried out anonymously, in remembrance of the Beatle who, from the bed in this suite, urged the world to give peace a chance.

The Hilton Amsterdam Hotel may be credited with housing the first 'bed-in' for Lennon and his new wife, Yoko Ono, but it is the Queen Elizabeth that would become inextricably linked to the couple's potent methods of protest, as it was here, during their week-long stay, that they recorded their restorative song of hope 'Give Peace a Chance'. With some basic studio equipment and a group of onlookers (including Allen Ginsberg, Petula Clark and Timothy Leary providing the backing vocals), the song was released just five weeks later and soon became synonymous with peaceful protest.

Not all, however, were impressed with Lennon's bed-in. Al Capp, the American cartoonist, proved to be a font of sarcasm and scathing criticism, for whom the idea of peaceful protest seemed anathema. His opening gambit when interviewing the couple during their bed-in was 'I'm a dreadful Neanderthal fascist'. It went downhill from there and ended with Lennon paraphrasing his own lyrics, singing: '… and they're gonna crucify Capp'.

Despite the dissenting few, continued worldwide adulation has meant that Lennon's message of peace, spoken from behind a curtain of hair while insulated between the bed sheets, has made Suite 1742 something of a rock 'n' roll landmark.

Unsurprisingly, it's now called the John Lennon and Yoko Ono Suite and features framed gold records, black-and-white photos of John and Yoko during the bed-in (taken by photographer Gerry Deiter for *Life* magazine) and other related memorabilia. Thankfully, the hotel hasn't succumbed to hippy affectation and swamped the suite with joss sticks and mock peace signs. Instead, this executive suite is underpinned with crimson carpeting and has been lent an elegant slant by virtue of the splashes of beige and caramel, typical of the hotel's rooms. The suite does not feature the actual bed used for the bed-in, but you can be assured that it's a luxurious king-sized one.

The famous suite is not the Queen Elizabeth's most opulent offering, though. Legend has it that John and Yoko turned up at the Queen Elizabeth without any money; the hotel just put them up on the 17th floor (some enterprising manager probably knew what future revenues such a public guest might generate) and Apple Records footed the bill at a later date. Had John and Yoko been carrying some serious cash in their pyjama pockets they may have opted for one of the larger suites. The Mont-Royal Suite, for example, is more befitting of a rock star. Installed on the top floor, this penthouse apartment consists of a sizeable living room and a bedroom with marble bathroom, complete with jet tub, while a connecting guest room is available upon request.

Ultimately, the Fairmont is all about Suite 1742 – a USP that has lead the hotel to occasionally run Bed-in for Peace packages. Additionally, if you want to make the grand entrance with all the incandescence of a rock star, you could join the Fairmont President's Club. This self-described 'recognition programme' enables guests to check in via a private reception desk (in other words you can check in – and get into some pyjamas – quicker than everybody else).

Fairmont The Queen Elizabeth, 900 Rene Levesque Boulevard West, Montréal, Québec H3B 4A5, Canada

(+1) 514 861 3511
queenelizabeth.hotel@fairmont.com
www.fairmont.com/queenelizabeth

SEE

JUST FOR LAUGHS

2101 Saint-Laurent Boulevard, Montréal, Québec H2X 2T5; www.justforlaughs.com and www.hahaha.com

Montréal is home to the world's biggest comedy festival. Running for a full month, each July, the festival hosts both local and international comedians. Past notable acts include: Tim Allen, Jerry Seinfeld, Bill Cosby, John Cleese, the cast of *The Simpsons* and *Family Guy*, and Flight of the Conchords. The festival also screens comedy films. So, if you love your belly fit to burst with laughter, book yourself a ticket or two.

WALKING GHOST TOUR

Old Montréal; www.fantommontreal.com/en

For something on the dark side, join a walking tour of Old Montréal or the wharfs of the Old Port with a ghost guide. Discover the secrets of the city's dark and criminal past as you visit the locations of long-ago hangings, murders and witch hunts.

BE SEEN

MÉTROPOLIS

59 Sainte-Catherine Street East, Montréal, Québec H2X 1K5; www.montrealmetropolis.ca

A performing arts centre, Métropolis is the premier music venue in Montréal. As well as being able to hold up to 2,300 music fans, it also has a lounge area called Le Savoy, which hosts events and gigs for smaller acts. The venue has been witness to performances by artists ranging from Joss Stone to Coheed and Cambria.

PLAYHOUSE
5656 Avenue du Parc, Mile-End, Montréal, Québec H2V 4H1
Formerly a strip-club, this bar is now the place to hang out for local indie fans and students. Playing a mixture of punk, alternative, garage and psychobilly music, and hosting a range of local live bands, Playhouse should have something for everyone. With a central stage and mosh pit, its atmosphere is dark but energetic.

LE PARKER MERIDIEN

Picture the scene: Nikki Sixx, wayward bassist for the depraved Mötley Crüe, returns to his empty hotel room at Le Parker Meridien after a poor show. He sits staring at a bindle of smack. He knows he shouldn't. He knows it's killing him. He's only too aware of its potency. But he reasons that smack also makes sex last longer. He shoots up. His ravaged torso is found slumped on the floor by his mercurial girlfriend, Vanity, who lets out a shrill cry for help. Fred Saunders, the former Hell's Angel who is now Head of Security for the band, is alerted and Nikki is revived.

Despite his sallow appearance, Nikki continues with the scheduled shows and even manages to celebrate the band's New York performances with champagne, whisky and a few lines. Even though Nikki has only been in his hotel room a few days, the reverential space is now stained with blood and black hair dye, having witnessed an overdose, sex ('fucking several chicks', Nikki notes in his diary) and fighting. Remarkably, this hasn't derailed Sixx and his substance-induced theatrics, such as setting his whisky-soaked penis on fire and sawing his manager's bed in half, continue unabated.

Over the years, Le Parker Meridien has proved to be the place for musicians to swoon into and perform to the media minions: days before Mötley Crüe's sojourn at the hotel, Bon Jovi were here for a press conference, the interviews for which ended up on their *Slippery When Wet* 'rockumentary'. Three years earlier, Bono gave an interview to WBCN radio in Boston from his room on the 22nd floor during U2's 1984 tour and complained that he was unable to get out onto the street due to the swarm of fans outside. Flocks of fans are not confined to the likes of U2; a milling throng craning their necks in the hope of catching a glimpse of the source of their affection is a regular feature outside the hotel.

For those wishing to kick bad habits, the hotel's Gravity Fitness Centre offers cardio conditioning, strength training, personal training, a spa and a nutritionist. Plus, even if you don't dip your toes in, take in the breathtaking view of Manhattan from the rooftop pool before plummeting back to the ground floor for a drink or the best coffee in midtown at the hotel's Knave bar. Even though the bar actually sits in a passageway, between the entrance at 118 West 57th Street and the 56th Street lobby, the large domed ceilings and swathes of red curtains create the feel of a gothic citadel. One of the hotel's preeminent features, for locals and tourists alike, is the burger joint (turn left at the concierge desk). Here, you can sample one of the best burgers in the Big Apple; the celebrity signatures covering the exposed brick wall lay testament to such a claim.

In contrast to the plush ground floor, the hotel's rooms feel positively minimal, albeit with the most spectacular views of Central Park. There's a variety of suites to choose from; each one takes on the guise of a swanky New York apartment.

And those of you who are still 'big kids' will think that the Le Parker Meridien has the coolest lifts. The *Tom & Jerry* and *Laurel & Hardy* movies being played within will no doubt see many a guest miss their floor as they try to catch the whole show.

Le Parker Meridien Hotel, 119 West 56th Street, New York, NY 10019, USA

(+1) 212 245 5000
reservations@parkermeridien.com
www.parkermeridien.com

SEE

FIFTH AVENUE

Lined with all of the premier retail stores (Tiffany & Co, Versace, Prada and again, for those 'big kids', there's the Disney Store), Fifth Avenue is regarded as being one of the most expensive streets in the world. As well as being a haven for shoppers, Fifth Avenue offers an address to many famous landmarks: the Empire State Building, Rockefeller Center, the New York Public Library as well as a wealth of museums (the Solomon R. Guggenheim Museum, Museum of the City of New York and Metropolitan Museum of Art, to name a few).

ARTISTS & FLEAS

70 North 7th Street, Williamsburg, Brooklyn, NY 11211;
www.artistsandfleas.com
Part vintage clothing/collectibles, part showcase for emerging/indie artists and part community gathering, this unique and friendly indoor market is bound to have you falling in love with something retro here. It's open every weekend.

BE SEEN

THE BOWERY BALLROOM

6 Delancey Street, Manhattan, New York, NY 10002;
www.boweryballroom.com
An intimate venue (capacity is just 550) that puts on the latest buzz bands, such as Mumford & Sons, as well as heavy legendaries including The Melvins. Suffice to say, it's a venue at which you always feel close to the action. If you're of small stature, however, you'll be better off seating yourself in the upstairs area where none of the intimacy is lost. Or simply grab one of the leather couches in the downstairs bar.

CAKE SHOP

152 Ludlow Street, Manhattan, New York, NY 10002;
www.cake-shop.com
Many things rolled into one, the Cake Shop serves freshly brewed coffee and vegan cupcakes, and is a record store with over 10,000

Le Parker Meridien

LPs for vinyl enthusiasts. Downstairs, you will also find a live music bar. Sit in a church pew and catch the latest tunes from local garage, punk and rock bands.

THE HOTEL CHELSEA

—◦◦◦◦◦—

'I remember you well in the Chelsea Hotel… Giving me head on the unmade bed,' crooned Leonard Cohen in 1974, recalling his affair with Janis Joplin. If Cohen were to stand in front of the Chelsea today, he would probably recollect his heady days with equally acute poetic abandon, as time has done little to alter the hotel's Draconian-Gothic exterior.

When scanning upwards to the top 12th storey of red brick, interspersed with wrought-iron balconies and a tacky neon sign clinging to the side, it's easy to feel somewhat underwhelmed. Nevertheless, the hotel's real lure is its impressive history. A host of luminaries has swaggered through the doors, from William Burroughs and the Beatniks of the 50s, right up to contemporary icons such as Madonna. In fact, some even took up long-term residence here: Arthur Miller stayed for six years, during which time he wrote *Incident at Vichy*, *After the Fall* and *The Price*; Bob Dylan lived in Suite 2011; Thomas Wolfe wrote *You Can't Go Home Again* in Room 829; and Dylan Thomas drank himself to death in Room 205. But you won't be able to see Room 100, the room in which Sid Vicious is said to have stabbed his girlfriend Nancy Spungen to death in 1978, as it no longer exists – asking reception staff about it results in much rolling of the eyes (though maybe they were just having a bad day at the time…). It would seem that out of all the tragedies the Chelsea has encountered, it is only the Vicious/Spungen murder case that the hotel appears keen to eradicate from its chequered past. Indeed, the hotel's previous proprietor, Stanley Bard (who ran the place for over 50 years), was famously disdainful of the brutal incident, often refusing to talk about the murderous event altogether.

The Hotel Chelsea

The hotel's interior does nothing to dispel the famed tales of bohemian life. It is as unique as the exterior is forbidding. A staircase in reception winds its way past an array of original artwork – all of it donated by past and present tenants. Elsewhere, an eclectic mix of furniture emits a sense of faded splendour. Saunter down the sombre corridors, glimpse the peculiar architecture and you'll find ragged glamour pervades, almost as though the Chelsea's management has tried to freeze-frame the hotel at its decadent zenith.

And, well, it kind of works. There is certainly an aura of licentious artistry that may well incite you to follow your own hedonistic inclinations, as many a great artisan has done while ensconced here. Besides, there is little else to do; there is no gym, swimming pool or games room. It is a hotel where creating an atmosphere conducive to creativity is more important than fitting rooms out in a luxurious fashion. Indeed, film-makers should note that the Chelsea welcomes filming projects, stating that 'the staff are production-friendly, ready to assist with delivery of equipment and wardrobes'. The Chelsea also claims that at least two films a year are shot at the hotel; past films that have utilised its unique atmosphere include *9¹/₂ Weeks*, *Leon* and Andy Warhol's *Chelsea Girls*.

Step into any of the 250 rooms and it's like walking onto a film set, albeit one for a horror movie. Floor-to-ceiling windows throw light across worn fabric and shabby walls as the whole room creaks under tired floorboards.

Despite its eccentric charm, the allure of the Chelsea may soon be lost among those of a bohemian disposition. Recent management changes have meant that creative vagrants can no longer stay for as long as they want. In fact, the maximum stay allowed is just 21 days, which has caused unrest among some of the hotel's long-term residents, as they fear they will soon be nudged out to make way for the more transient visitor. The

14

otel's new owners ousted previous manager, Bard, who was
regarded as more of a lenient landlord for counterculture artists.
Though, for now, the Chelsea still stands at a defiant distance
from the gentrification offered by most hotels. No two rooms
are the same and each one seems to exude its own spirit,
ensuring every visit is unique, should you choose to stay more
than once.

Some may be a bit perturbed by the Chelsea's tattered
features, but there's no denying its ability to capture the
admiration of many a free spirit. Arthur Miller once observed
that 'there are no vacuum cleaners, no rules and shame'. It is no
surprise, then, that the Chelsea is both a cultural institution and
the haunting ground for the ghost of Sid Vicious, looking for
his stabbed girlfriend. The latter being just a possibility, of
course.

**The Hotel Chelsea, 222 West 23rd Street, Manhattan, New
York, NY 10011, USA**

+1) 212 243 3700
reservations@hotelchelsea.com
www.hotelchelsea.com

SEE

STRAWBERRY FIELDS

Central Park, Manhattan, New York; see www.centralpark.com
This 2½-acre teardrop-shaped section of Central Park has been dedicated to the memory of John Lennon, shot while entering the Dakota apartment block across the street in 1980. Yoko Ono gave a million dollars for the landscaping and maintenance of the park. Fans hold vigils there every year on the date of Lennon's birthday (9 October).

ED SULLIVAN THEATER

1697–1699 Broadway, Manhattan, New York, NY 10019
This radio and television studio has been used as a venue for live and recorded broadcasts since 1936. Ed Sullivan is famous not just for his variety show but also for banning Bo Diddley, Buddy Holly, The Byrds, The Rolling Stones and The Doors for 'raucous' behaviour or inappropriate lyrics.

BE SEEN

VILLAGE UNDERGROUND

130 West 3rd Street, Manhattan, New York, NY 10012;
www.thevillageunderground.com
Described as the most dynamic live music venue in New York, the VU has a party every night of the week. With a range of open-mic nights, jamming sessions, DJs, belly dancing and a house band playing vintage rock and world/country music, there's never a dull moment.

ROSELAND BALLROOM

239 West 52nd Street, Manhattan, New York, NY 10019;
www.roselandballroom.com
This quirky venue has hosted everything from Hilary Clinton's birthday party to movie premieres and is a regular spot for gigs by the likes of AC/DC, Madonna, Nirvana and The Rolling Stones.

STONOVER FARM

Your diligent host has just served up a selection of cheeses, together with some wine. After sampling fromageophile delights and having engaged in some light conversation with fellow amiable guests, you retreat to a cushioned window seat to gaze out at the large expanse of manicured lawns that merge into the lush green of the woods. You allow yourself to be transported to a place of mental calm, far from the toil and bustle of everyday life. As dusk embraces the serenity, you wish you could distil the experience so that you may take a piece of this tranquillity home with you.

Now that doesn't sound very rock 'n' roll. Admittedly, Stonover doesn't have a lurid history peppered with casualties. In fact, Stonover isn't even a hotel; it's a B&B. And yes, as with most B&Bs, once you've sleepily wended your way down to breakfast, you'll find the buoyant owner masquerading as chef and cooking your morning omelette. Only the buoyant owner in question happens to be Tom Werman – esteemed record producer for the likes of Mötley Crüe, Poison, Blue Öyster Cult, Ted Nugent and Twisted Sister, among others.

Tom Werman has stated that Stonover is, in fact, the 'anti-B&B'; you won't find an abundance of antique furniture and floral patterns here. Under the aegis of Tom and his wife Suky, Stonover offers sleekly refined accommodation where muted hues predominate and the amenities are on a par with those of a distinguished city hotel.

Charting a new course in the world of B&Bs, Stonover Farm has three suites and two separate buildings. All of the suites are kitted out with entertainment armoires and a substantial collection of music, as you'd expect. In Suite 1 let the large two-headed shower and deep-soaking tub dissolve any stress and anxiety from your body; or choose Suite 2, the largest suite, for its well-appointed sitting room with generous views of the woods. The suitably named Rock Cottage bears all the charm of a country inn, furnished, as it is, with stone fireplace and hardwood floors. The flagship accommodation, however, is the cosy School House with its glorious underfloor heating. Here you'll find a main room, bedroom (with king-sized bed) and bathroom with jacuzzi and, outside, its own patio.

If all this talk of genteel cheese and wine evenings in placid surroundings seems a little incongruous, then take heed of the fact that Stonover has what a lot of rock 'n' roll hotels don't have: a first-hand account of the sort of tales that are often fabricated by effusive myth makers, keen to make their stories the stuff of legend. But Tom Werman can percolate the truth from the myth. So, as you seat yourself for breakfast muffins, take the time to broach the subjects of jamming with Jimi Hendrix, working at Epic Records, overseeing the soundtrack for the film *Rock Star* and having 25 Gold and Platinum records. Plus, having managed to abstain from the dissipation of the rock world while those around him exhausted all hedonistic possibilities, Tom has a lucid account of what actually happened on the depraved fringe. Therefore, to get the real dirt on rock music's favourite delinquents, Mötley Crüe, (Tom produced the albums 'Shout at the Devil', 'Theatre of Pain' and 'Girls, Girls, Girls') this B&B owner is the go-to raconteur. Although, Tom will admit that, when it comes to the 'world's most notorious band', life for the band really was a giddy mix of sex, drugs and rock 'n' roll: 'They weren't pretending. They're great guys, but they lived fast and hard, no question about it'.

Having been at the helm for over 60 records, Tom ceded the producer's chair in LA and moved east to Lenox, after reading a motivational book entitled *Who Moved My Cheese?*

(Are you sensing a theme here?) Having digested the business fable, Tom made the transformation from consummate heavy metal producer to B&B proprietor. Still, Tom hasn't totally expunged himself from his rock 'n' roll past: he wrote to *The New York Times Book Review*, disputing some of the disparaging comments made about him by Nikki Sixx in his memoir *The Heroin Diaries*.

Given that Tom was probably sober and clear-headed at the time, you'll probably want to side with his version of things. Bet that evening of cheese and wine doesn't seem so sedate now, eh?

Stonover Farm, 169 Under Mountain Road, Lenox, MA 01240, USA

(+1) 413 637 9100
stonoverfarm@aol.com
www.stonoverfarm.com

SEE

TANGLEWOOD MUSIC FESTIVAL
Tanglewood, MA 01240; see www.bso.org
Set on a 100-acre estate with a 5,000-seat amphitheatre, Tanglewood Music Festival puts on shows throughout the summer. A whole range of music genres are catered to, including the likes of James Taylor and Linda Ronstadt making appearances alongside the Boston Symphony Orchestra and jazz legend Herbie Hancock.

FURNACE BROOK WINERY
508 Canaan Road, Richmond, MA 01254;
www.furnacebrookwinery.com
Just 10 miles from Lenox, this family-run winery is located on a 100-year-old farm. After your free wine sampling, you can relax by the fire with even more wine or some hot cider. Alternatively, take a stroll through the orchard or explore the back-country trails around the winery.

BE SEEN

OLDE HERITAGE TAVERN
12 Housatonic Street, Lenox, MA 01240
With Lenox proving to be the rural retreat for affluent families, it can often be tricky to find a bar that is a bit more casual. So, if you're looking for somewhere easy-going, this place is a little gem: Guinness from the tap, good food and a pool table, to boot.

PEARL STREET NIGHTCLUB
10 Pearl Street, Northampton, MA 01060;
www.iheg.com/pearl_street_main.asp
With both a ballroom and a club room, this venue hosts a variety of events. Rockers such as Dark Star Orchestra have played here, and events such as Battle of the Bands, indie/punk theme nights, music shows and salsa dances happen regularly.

COMFORT INN DOWNTOWN

If there were an award for 'The Hotel that had been Privy to the Most Debauchery', this Comfort Inn – formerly Swingos Celebrity Inn – would be a strong contender for the gong, alongside, maybe, Chateau Marmont (see page 45) and the Andaz West Hollywood (see page 57). Excluding LA hotels, though, it would be a sure winner.

Swingos' notorious reputation began in earnest when Elvis sashayed into the unprepossessing hotel having booked over 100 rooms spread over three floors. By the time the King checked out, with a $20,000 hotel bill, the hotel's fate had been decided. Before long, word spread among the bands, managers and tour promoters that Swingos was hosting the perennial party. From 1971, this hotel endured a rock 'n' roll feast that lasted a little over a decade and was attended by an army of consummate revellers: The Rolling Stones, The Doors, The Eagles, The Allman Brothers Band, Kiss, Aerosmith, Queen, Pink Floyd, Deep Purple and The Clash are just some of the bands that rolled up to this downtown hotel for some voracious partying.

Then, there are those who really ramped up the debauchery. Known for his whirlwind personality as much as his frantic drumming, Keith Moon's reputation as hotel deleaguerer preceded him. Most knew of the infamous antics that included, among other things, blowing up toilets with maniacal glee. But Swingos was not one for turning the destructive appetites away. It's not so much that they turned a blind eye (how do you ignore Lynyrd Skynyrd swinging from a chandelier?) as much as they simply flexed their way through the ensuing mayhem with a tenacity that matched the destructive urges of the bands they were welcoming. And so, with bated breath, the hotel welcomed a Keith Moon dressed as a cop and watched as he proceeded to handcuff two strangers together. Incidentally, there were no reports of lavatory porcelain being reduced to dust or of furniture being nailed to ceilings. Almost certainly, then, this would have been a moment in which hotel management was thankful for small mercies.

But another rock 'n' roll tornado that just couldn't be reckoned with lay on the horizon. In 1977, Led Zeppelin checked in. Now, as any dyed-in-the-wool rock fan will know, having these hardy debauchees take a few rooms could mean your hotel was about to be left beyond repair. Nevertheless, the fact that the band had an accountant in tow seemed to salve fears for hotel management. (Still, if ever there were a harbinger of hotel trashing, then a rock band travelling with an accountant to tally up costs of damages would be the surest sign that your hotel was about undergo some serious destruction.) Led Zeppelin checked out paying $13,000 for damages.

The cracks have long since been filled in, the hotel has been rebranded, and if there are rock stars checking in here, they're certainly not in bands that are in the defenestration game, as the Comfort Inn has managed to maintain composure for a few decades now. Seemingly, the rock gods of yesteryear designed the template and then blew it to smithereens, and now all that's left are memories and stories for those who want to be regaled with tales of reckless living.

Although, that in itself might be tricky, as Ian Hunter from Mott the Hoople said: 'Swingos was a place you remember checking in and out of, but you can't remember anything in between'.

Comfort Inn Downtown, 1800 Euclid Avenue, Cleveland, OH 44115, USA

(+1) 216 861 0001
hotelhelp@choicehotels.com
www.comfortinn.com

SEE

ROCK AND ROLL HALL OF FAME AND MUSEUM
1100 Rock and Roll Boulevard, Cleveland, OH 44114;
www.rockhall.com
With active exhibitions, gigs, intimate photography, 3D concert footage and talks, this is more than just a museum. It is a must-see attraction. Spread over seven floors and five theatres, the Hall of Fame chronicles rock 'n' roll's illustrious history, recognising the major players and honouring the legends. Come and have the best music lesson of your life. Hello Cleveland, indeed.

HISTORIC WAREHOUSE DISTRICT
Cleveland; www.warehousedistrict.org
Within walking distance of the Rock and Roll Hall of Fame, Cleveland's first neighbourhood and oldest commercial district is home to more than 70 historical buildings. A hub of trendy restaurants, clubs and galleries, this area is well worth a stroll around – just don't forget the plastic.

BE SEEN

BEACHLAND BALLROOM
15711 Waterloo Road, Cleveland, OH 44110;
www.beachlandballroom.com
Just east of downtown, this hip venue – comprised of a ballroom and a tavern – hosts everything from pop to punk; folk to funk, rock and blues. The unique venue (the ballroom really is a ballroom, complete with decorative high ceiling) is popular for its great staff serving good food, and pulls in a fun-loving crowd for an entertaining night out.

PEABODY'S
2045 East 21st Street, Cleveland, OH 44115; www.peabodys.com
Originally converted from warehouse space and known as the
Pirate's Cove until the birth of Peabody's in 1982, this venue is
legendary for its rock 'n' roll resume. Artists as diverse as Pearl Jam,
R.E.M. and Bo Diddley have all played here – in fact, anyone who's
anyone.

THE EDGEWATER

~~◦✕✕✕✕◦~~

Originally conceived as a temporary structure to attract visitors to 1962's World Fair, the Edgeware Inn, as it was then known, defied its short-term purpose by remaining open for a further two years, until it hit its lowest commercial point, with its owners resigning themselves to the fact that the number of empty rooms would soon spell the hotel's demise. Indeed, it was anticipated that the Edgeware would not be known for its longevity and that Don Wright, the manager at the time, would be the last to oversee the edifice as a hotel.

Then, on 21 August 1964, The Beatles checked in. Despite their short stay, having The Fab Four booked in created a veritable buzz about the Edgeware, setting it upon a rock 'n' roll trajectory that would see an upswing in its fortune, attracting the likes of The Beach Boys, Ray Charles and The Rolling Stones.

So, why did The Beatles choose this seemingly unpopular hotel? Well, in short, no other hotel in Seattle would take them. It's difficult to imagine now, but back then hotels would have looked askance at these mop-tops, even though they were hardly the most notorious rock 'n' roll musicians. The Edgeware, however, had nothing to lose.

In recognition of The Beatles' inadvertent succour, Room 272 (the room the famous quartet shared) is now The Beatles Suite, resplendent with the requisite paraphernalia: Beatles CDs, portraits, books and, perhaps most intriguing of all, a photo of the four Liverpudlians fishing from the hotel window, their rods cast out into Seattle's Elliot Bay. The famous shot was taken at a time when fishing from hotel windows was permitted.

But then Led Zeppelin came to stay. Managing to fuse fishing with sex and rock 'n' roll, Zeppelin gave the owners good reason to give the hotel's angling feature a rethink. Known as the 'fish incident' or 'mud shark episode', the story of Led Zeppelin's infamous stay has been contorted over the years, leaving a trail of contradictions in its wake. But Zeppelin's Road Manager, Richard Cole, in the definitive Led Zeppelin biography *Hammer of the Gods* claims it was not a shark but rather a red snapper that was inserted into a groupie's vagina. 'It was nothing malicious,' states Cole, going on to declare 'she must have come 20 times'.

Depraved marine appetites aside, this rock-star-endorsed hotel isn't just for those with profligate lives. The archetypal north-west style makes for a relaxed environment and that laidback vibe pervades throughout. The high-beamed ceilings and pine furniture in the rustic lobby create a restful pastoral setting from which to enjoy the sight of the majestic Olympic Mountains. Apart from the 'cityside' rooms, all suites come furnished with gas fireplaces, commanding views of the bay and the type of knotted-wood furniture you'd expect to find in a snug retreat deep in the wilderness. Even The Beatles Suite has splashes of lodgepole bark amid all the 60s memorabilia.

But if all this is beginning to sound a bit too bucolic then, rest-assured, the hotel is still keen to prove that it can accommodate any rock 'n' roll aficionado. Choose the Penthouse Suite or The Beatles Suite and you will find that the modern has been embraced too; both suites offer state-of-the-art stereo systems, designer lighting, leather sofas and, of course, the knock-out views. The palatial Penthouse Suite is split over two levels; and with two huge plasma HD TVs, whirlpool tub and a four-post king-sized bed, it definitely has the decadent edge. Add the his 'n' her sinks and a shower bathed in the red glow emanating from the hotel's illuminated 'E' sign, and you're bound to consider it to be one of the more opulent suites you've had the pleasure to stay in.

As you may expect from a building that seems to hover just above the water, the hotel's restaurant, too, boasts arresting views of Seattle's Elliot Bay and Olympic Mountains. If you get the chance, dine out on the patio and enjoy the delicious Pacific north-west cuisine.

It's a shame that there's no fishing out of the windows these days, but if you do want to snag a room with the same sea views afforded to The Beatles and Led Zeppelin then make sure you choose a 'waterfront' and not a 'waterside' room. You may just be able to spot the occasional relieved-looking snapper in the waters below.

The Edgewater Hotel, 2411 Alaskan Way, Pier 67, Seattle, WA 98121, USA

(+1) 206 728 7000
reservations@edgewaterhotel.com
www.edgewaterhotel.com

The Edgewater

SEE

EXPERIENCE MUSIC PROJECT
Seattle Center, 325 5th Avenue North, Seattle, WA 98109;
www.empsfm.org
The EMP is a must-visit for those truly into music. It describes itself
as a 'music museum combining interactive and interpretive exhibits
to tell the story of the creative, innovative and rebellious expression
that defines American popular music'. There's a cool collection of
Jimi Hendrix memorabilia too.

SPACE NEEDLE
400 Broad Street, Seattle, WA 98109; www.spaceneedle.com
Think Seattle, and three things come to mind – rain, coffee and the
Space Needle. Head straight for the SkyCity restaurant, which really
does move through 360° and sits over 150 metres (500 feet) up,
giving you the most spectacular views of the city. Past stars who've
stopped by include Elvis Presley, John Travolta, Claudia Schiffer and
Melanie Griffiths, as you film buffs out there will probably know.

BE SEEN

BELLTOWN
On Seattle's downtown waterfront; www.belltown.org
Seattle has a rich music scene and artists such as Nirvana, Pearl Jam,
Soundgarden, Alice in Chains and Mudhoney all called it 'home'.
Head to Belltown where all the famous venues, such as the
Crocodile Café and Dimitriou's Jazz Alley, that helped give birth to
grunge still remain.

EASY STREET RECORDS & CAFÉ
4559 California Avenue South West, Seattle, WA 98116;
www.easystreetonline.com
A great place to browse for undiscovered music, order something
different from knowledgeable and friendly staff, enjoy an espresso
and waffle, blast your hangover with a greasy breakfast or enjoy
some in-store entertainment, such as live sets from up-and-coming
bands.

WHITE EAGLE

Now, when you check into a place called The White Eagle Café, Saloon and Rock 'n' Roll Hotel, to give the hotel it's full title, you must surely have an inkling of what lies in store. The InterContinental, it is not.

If the name of this hotel, carved into a large wooden sign jutting out above its saloon doors, conjures up images of amoral gun-slingers fighting it out in the Wild West, then you're not too far off the mark when it comes to this hotel's history. Nicknamed the Bucket of Blood, due to all the bloody altercations that once took place here, the White Eagle Saloon opened in the early 1900s for the roustabouts that worked down at the docks who would come here to play poker, get drunk and either sate their addictions in the opium den downstairs or go about their indecorous ways in the brothel upstairs. Legend has it that the latter 'service' resulted in the death of a prostitute who, according to White Eagle lore, was murdered by a jealous lover.

Thankfully, there's no fresh blood on the history books and the 11 rooms that make up the hotel have long since been renovated. The saloon, however, the oldest in this industrial part of town, has retained an aura that exudes an outlaw sensibility harking back to its bloody history: the silhouetted white eagle painted on the outside of the hotel has been captured mid flight, wings spread, hovering like some harbinger of lawlessness. Of course, you're not about to be caught in any crossfire – this is the north-west and not the American south-west, after all – but you might feel as though you've walked on to the set for a Sergio Leone movie as you get close to the hotel's dusty facade.

Step inside and you'll find that the White Eagle has a vintage oak bar, which may seem somewhat incongruous due to the distinct lack of ragtag fugitives chewing toothpicks and smoking stogies dipped in whisky. However, you'll quickly surmise that there is scant reason to expect any unruly behaviour; in fact, you're more likely to be asked whether you fancy anything from the menu (which offers good pub fare, by the way) than you are to be challenged to a brawl for throwing a glance in the wrong direction.

The White Eagle might still keep a sticky barnacle tethered to its desperado past, but the hotel is not so deeply rooted in its history that it doesn't have a beady eye on the present. Proving that it's above flophouse status, by night the White Eagle turns into a buzzing live music venue, supporting local acts at nightly gigs and helping newcomers find their feet on the open-mic nights.

Live music is not a new venture for the White Eagle, but a defining attribute that has been in place since the 1970s; and it's this spirit that has enabled the hotel to 'let the good times roll'. Well, once you've managed to attract notable musicians, such as Grammy-award-winner Robert Cray, to your tiny venue, you can add the words 'Rock 'n' Roll' to your hotel name with complete confidence. In fact, blues legend Cray didn't just show up for a quick set – he helped the White Eagle become a venue of enviable repute by playing there regularly.

Now, following Cray's famed performances, stories of a different kind sprung up: eager revellers queuing up to gain entry, even in the early hours of the morning; bands spending their gig fee on 125 shots of tequila for the audience; and Hollywood actors (Matt Dillon) and hirsute rockers (Billy Gibbons from ZZ Top) dropping by for a drink – which is no mean feat for a small saloon with a corner stage and a few rooms you can crash in for as little as $40 a night.

The only thing you may wish to take heed of, if you're a light sleeper, is that your bed is essentially above a music venue. And, if that doesn't keep you awake, then the restless spirit of the murdered lady of the night will. Only joking; but if you are concerned about hearing anything that could give you the jitters, then down a few Burning Furnace cocktails at the bar before retiring to bed and no banshee has a chance in hell of waking you.

White Eagle Saloon & Hotel, 836 North Russell Street, Portland, OR 97227, USA

(+1) 503 335 8900
eagle@mcmenamins.com
www.mcmenamins.com

SEE

PORTLAND AERIAL TRAM
3303 South West Bond Avenue, Portland, OR 97239;
www.portlandtram.org
Get a ticket to ride in this cable-car-esque tram from alongside the Willamette River up to Marquam Hill, with far-out views of the city. Not for those with vertigo.

HOPWORKS URBAN BREWERY
2944 South East Powell Boulevard, Portland, OR 97202;
www.hopworksbeer.com
Not content with being Portland's first eco-brew pub, with outstanding beers and the thinnest, crispiest pizzas, HUB also has a 'bar bike' – its one-of-a-kind design holds kegs of beer below a wooden bar with a rack to hold pizza, plus it has its own compact sound system. As befits the USA's greenest city, everything here is organic. And the menu is pretty varied, too. Beer cheese soup, anyone?

BE SEEN

CRYSTAL BALLROOM
1332 West Burnside, Portland, OR 97209; www.mcmenamins.com
James Brown, Grateful Dead, Blue Cheer and Frank Zappa have all played at this classic ballroom. The venue continues to pull in the punters with its booking policy, but the other draw for crowds is the restaurant and the 'floating' dancefloor. Also, the main ballroom is replete with classic floor-to-ceiling arches, high ceilings and glinting chandeliers, making this a unique music venue.

BENSON HOTEL
309 Southwest Broadway, Portland, OR 97205;
www.bensonhotel.com
If you fancy an evening in even more awe-inspiring surroundings, then head to this decadently charged hotel to sit back at its swanky bar and take in the lavish setting that attracts celebrities and rock stars alike.

HOTEL MARK TWAIN

Rock 'n' roll hotel rooms often seem to fall into one of two camps. First, those that have been elegantly adorned with all the grandeur of a royal palace, equipped with every grown-up toy and attracting the big Hollywood players whose every demanding whim is anticipated by assiduously attentive staff. Then, there is camp two, with their rusty furniture and musty air, providing accommodation that could be considered way below par, but that nevertheless possesses tangible character, where the scantiness of luxury is overcome by notoriety and infamy. In short, having a debauched tale to tell usually means hoteliers hold onto the decrepit furnishings in an attempt to hang onto the final breath that weakly left some rock star's lungs, thus entrenching their hotel's two-star status in the annals of rock history and firmly on the pilgrims' rock 'n' roll map.

Measured by either yardstick, Room 203 of Mark Twain's namesake hotel would fare pretty badly. It is, by anyone's standards, a pedestrian affair: subdued hues frame a modest space consisting of a simple wooden desk, bedside table and a couple of beds with unprepossessing headboards. Unpretentious and comfortable, it neither overwhelms nor underwhelms, but merely exists without the slightest hint that anything amiss ever took place here. Only a newspaper clipping and the plaque on the room's door lifts it above the anonymity afforded to the other rooms. It reads simply: 'Billie Holiday occupied this suite on January 22nd 1949'.

On that fateful night, federal narcotics agents raided the hotel room Holiday was sharing with her manager-boyfriend, John Levy, and seized a stash of opium. Holiday was arrested and it was a case of Lady sings the Blues. A week before she

33

was due in court, Holiday was beaten by Levy who also took her money and her fur coat. Holiday stood in the dock wearing tired-looking clothes and sporting a black eye. Having always kept a retinue of dealers – Levy was the third drug addict she had dated and was thought to have framed her in said drugs bust – it was not the first time she had been arrested for drugs (she was jailed in 1947 for heroin possession) but the famous jazz chanteuse's lifestyle was beginning to leave indelible marks on her. Ten years later, after sustained drug abuse, she would die of liver and heart disease.

A portrait of Holiday, with her deep-red bow lips, slightly parted as if to attempt a smile, and heavy-lidded yet beaming eyes, hangs in the lobby. Next to this beautiful rendering of Holiday's sultry grace is a portrait of Mark Twain in his later years, all snowy haired and surly looking with a thick moustache. They make an odd couple, side-by-side, pinned against the back wall behind the reception desk overseeing guests check-in; though you can easily see why it is the Leading Lady of Jazz that has earned the most doting of tributes – poet Frank O'Hara penned the ode 'The Day Lady Died', U2 wrote 'Angel of Harlem' and the United States Postal Service put her face on a postage stamp. And yet, aside from the portrait and the namesake suite, there's not a hint of Holiday's jazz glamour when it comes to the decor of the hotel.

Instead, as you might expect given the hotel's name, it is Mark Twain or, rather, the era in which Mark Twain lived, that sets the tone. The briefest of ambles round the building will demonstrate how the hotel alludes to what Twain referred to as 'The Gilded Age' (circa 1869–1889). Well, sort of. We're talking brass rails, custard-yellow walls, plantation shutters and dark exotic woods; but, nevertheless, there's a distinct feel of the late 19th century. The Holiday Suite, though, is far from being the most lavish room in the hotel.

Which perhaps gives us a third camp in which to place hotel rooms: a category in which the wholesomeness of the setting belies the notoriety. Such rooms are just as endearing: they leave more to the imagination, feed the myths and, in turn, keep the legends alive in the minds of music lovers.

Hotel Mark Twain, 345 Taylor Street, San Francisco, CA 94102, USA

+1) 415 673 2332
reservations@hotelmarktwain.com
www.hotelmarktwain.com

SEE

JEFFERSON AIRPLANE HOUSE
2400 Fulton Street, San Francisco, CA 94118
The band bought this 20-room mansion, opposite Golden Gate Park, in 1968. Then, they painted it black and made it the hub for both musical and recreational activity. It was home to Jefferson Airplane's own studio and legendary parties as well as a large number of stray cats. These days it's been repainted but you can still stand there, gaze up and picture the circus of hippies who languidly stepped past its Doric columns into a kaleidoscopic sanctuary. If it is hard to imagine, then try standing there while listening to Jefferson Airplane's Greatest Hits album, titled '2400 Fulton Street'.

GRATEFUL DEAD HOUSE
710 Ashbury Street, San Francisco, CA 94117
Grateful Dead lived here and made it their headquarters between October 1966 and March 1968. In October 1967, police raided the band's house with reporters and TV cameras in tow. Members of the group were arrested for possession of marijuana and the incident earned itself coverage in the first edition of *Rolling Stone* magazine.

Hotel Mark Twain

BE SEEN

ROCKIT ROOM
406 Clement Street, San Francisco, CA 94118;
www.rock-it-room.com
Upstairs in the Rockit Room, with its top-notch sound system, is the place to hear up-and-coming local and international bands on Fridays and Saturdays. Although geared towards live rock music, the venue also has open-mic and acoustic sessions during the week, a comedy night and a club night. What's more, downstairs there's a bar, pool table, impressive jukebox and lounge areas.

RED DEVIL LOUNGE
1695 Polk Street, San Francisco, CA 94109;
www.reddevillounge.com
Converted from a historic theatre to a saucy music club, this venue is known for its friendly atmosphere and strong drinks. In an environment of red lanterns and gold decor, the club hosts a wide range of bands, from Gene Loves Jezebel to the Human League.

PHOENIX

If you're the type of regular gig-goer who stands agog in the mosh pit, clinging onto the barrier to face a battery of Marshall amps firing out that powerful electric 'kerrang' guitar sound, you will be all too familiar with the shrill sound that rings in your ears long after the gig's decibels have ceased trying to pin you to the back wall.

Defective hearing is not confined to those experiencing the seismic assault out-front, either: those kicking out the jams on stage also receive deafening sidewinders. After years of performing with The Who, Pete Townshend cited continued exposure to the speakers erupting with his own cathartic riffs as the reason for his partial deafness and tinnitus. So, to save future rock 'n' roll trailblazers from the same fate, the veteran rocker became an advocate for the non-profit organisation Hearing Education and Awareness for Rockers (or HEAR for short), which has since become a philanthropic partner with the Phoenix Hotel's You Can Make a Difference programme.

The affiliation between HEAR and the Phoenix makes perfect sense given that this hotel is a sanctum for rock stars in San Francisco. Everyone apart from Mötley Crüe make up the motley crew listed in this hotel's guest registry. Take a deep breath: Little Richard, Linda Ronstadt, David Bowie, R.E.M., Red Hot Chili Peppers, Pearl Jam, Moby, The Psychedelic Furs, Vincent Gallo, Norah Jones, Maxïmo Park, The Killers, Bloc Party and The Shins have all bunked down in one of the 44 rooms that make up this small, but perfectly formed, boutique hotel.

Evidently, the title Rock 'n' Roll Hotel is no misnomer, then, given the impressive list of musical dignitaries and past visitors. But what is surprising about this is how the Phoenix has managed to herald this title from its location within a baleful area on the edge of the gone-to-seed Tenderloin neighbourhood of San Francisco. Sure, the hotel's close proximity to a number of music venues probably bolsters its popularity among touring musicians, but surely there has to be something else to consolidate its famed reputation, right? Well, one night here and you'll discover why: the nightlife is tantamount to the rock-star clientele. The hotel's Bambuddha Lounge, which manages to mix oriental influences with LA chic by way of attracting the hip echelon crowd to its bamboo domain, lets the young creatures of the night party full tilt until the early hours. And you'll probably find many of them the next day, staring vacantly at the oval pool and hanging around in abject states just in case Anthony Kiedis makes an appearance.

Before the Phoenix made its name it was known as the Caravan Lodge – a name befitting its motor lodge origins. As soon as you espy the hotel, you'll see that the Phoenix borrows heavily from its original 50s-era design: the hotel is a two-tiered building in which all the rooms have pastel-coloured doors and face a central courtyard – a layout typical of the 1950s motel. So, rather than take a wrecking ball to a slice of American history, they've utilised the space but got rid of the mid-century decor and added a modern touch, albeit with a pinch of the kitsch here and there: bamboo xylophones and artwork made from dead birds, anyone?

The 'dead bird' piece is actually a portrait of musician, actor and director Vincent Gallo. It was left outside his room by a smitten but surreptitious fan. Gallo had, apparently, wanted to take the portrait with him but couldn't fit the monstrous masterpiece into his car and so handed it over to the hotel who, in turn, added it to their own art collection, which now totals over 250 original pieces.

Furthermore, it would seem that the hotel's affiliation with the winged daemons of the sky goes beyond strange art pieces and the mythical fire bird from which it takes its name. In what ould have been pulled from a Hitchcock movie, emo-goth ockers My Chemical Romance had the ever-so ironic xperience of having their collective pallor attacked by a flock of lackbirds. The band's vocalist, Gerard Way, also claimed that as ney were leaving they saw the members from the metal band lipknot receiving the same vicious goodbye. Evidently, some ands have more to contend with than just tinnitus.

hoenix Hotel, 601 Eddy Street, San Francisco, CA 94109, 'SA

-1) 415 776 1380
oenixhotel@jdvhotels.com
ww.jdvhotels.com/hotels

SEE

CITY LIGHTS BOOKSTORE
261 Columbus Avenue, San Francisco, CA 94133;
www.citylights.com
Literature was closely aligned with 1960s counterculture; the work of the beat writers, in particular, was considered influential because of its liberal political slant. Founded by Lawrence Ferlinghetti, this bookstore, with its in-house publishing arm, gained notoriety when it chose to publish Allen Ginsberg's influential *Howl and Other Poems*, which consequently earned City Lights an obscenity trial. Thankfully the store has survived and still stocks seminal works of literature.

THE FILLMORE
1805 Geary Boulevard, San Francisco, CA 94115;
www.thefillmore.com
Like LA's Whisky a Go-Go (see page 43), the impact this San Fran venue had on the counterculture movement of the 60s is widely

acknowledged. Under the aegis of famous concert promoter Bill Graham, this venue hosted shows for legendary acts such as Grateful Dead and Jimi Hendrix. The Fillmore still puts on shows, but for a glimpse of it in its heyday (and to whet your appetite) search out the documentary film *Fillmore: The Last Days*, which documents the last run of shows under Graham's reign and features such luminaries as Santana, Hot Tuna and Jefferson Airplane.

BE SEEN

HEMLOCK TAVERN
1131 Polk Street, San Francisco, CA 94109;
www.hemlocktavern.com
With a highly adventurous booking policy, the Hemlock has played host to pop, garage, metal and rock bands. Savour the bags of hot peanuts or lodge yourself and your drink in the heated smoking lounge. The chilled-out atmosphere, strong drinks and DJ nights (punk rock on Mondays) all ensure a loyal and happy clientele.

CLUB DELUXE
1511 Haight Street, San Francisco, CA 94117;
www.sfclubdeluxe.com
For cocktails oozing the freshest of ingredients (try the Spa Collins), killer live bands, jazz musicians, comedy showcase nights (Mondays) and what has been called the best pizza in town, head for this quaint lounge. A breath of fresh air in a city of dark grungy pubs, you're sure to agree.

ALTA CIENEGA MOTEL

~~━━꙰ᎭᏞᎳᎦ━━~~

Prior to January 2011, when management changed hands, this was a Hollywood rock-star haunt markedly different from, say, the notorious Riot House or the Chateau Marmont (see page 45). The motel's insignia was set against an orange wall where a single light spilled a sickly glow, dimly lighting the way to a parking lot overlooked by a series of serried rooms, marked out only by their pallid yellow doors. In other words, it had all the hallmarks of an ominously isolated low-budget 40s-era motel – the sort that could be a movie set for a horror film in which the dated decor, scuffed carpets and broken deadbolts portended a sleepless night for hapless guests.

Yet, the motel no doubt had many benefits for Jim Morrison who, between 1968 and 1970, often holed out here.

Just across the road is Mexico y Barra Restaurant (previously the Benvenuto Café), which used to house the Doors' recording studio and offices. The 'men's room' in the restaurant was the vocal booth in which Morrison recorded tracks for the 'LA Woman' album. Also within close proximity is Barney's Beanery (see page 48) – a watering hole favoured by the dipsomaniacal vocalist – making Morrison's bed in Room 32 of the motel within staggering distance. Incidentally, Barney's was also a coveted spot for Janis Joplin, who was seen here in her favourite booth downing screwdrivers shortly before she retired to her room at the Landmark Hotel (now the Highland Gardens, see page 49) and overdosed on heroin.

Indeed, West Hollywood had a surfeit of musicians. When the Rolling Stones were in town to mix their 'Beggars Banquet' album, Mick Jagger reportedly paid Jim a visit at Alta Cienega Motel. Although, it should be mentioned that Jim rarely entertained guests at La Cienega; it was never the intention of his stay at the motel. Instead, the motel offered Morrison anonymity, allowing him space to become dislocated and stupefied in a cheap room and sleep off the effects of his heedless living. In truth, there wasn't – and still isn't – a lot else to do at Alta Cienega, as little has changed since Jim's sojourn here. The rooms might have been cleaned up, given a new lick of paint and had their scuffed carpets replaced as part of the upgrade completed by the new management, but they haven't lost too much of the affordable 40s-esque character that had lured Morrison in the first place.

And one room remains untouched. Room 32, the motel claims, is as Jim last saw it, with a bed, a bedside table and lamp, and a chair – that's it. It looks incredibly dated and forlorn. Incorrigible romantics who deem Morrison poet laureate of 1960s counterculture will love the place and may even feel inclined to leave an inscription expressing admiration for the Lizard King. The walls, the headboard and even the shower have been covered with graffiti – some of it poetic, some of it stolid – from the cavalcade of admirers who have been only too delighted to have used the same toilet as Jim Morrison. To all intents and purposes, it's a bit enervated. Tellingly, someone has scribbled 'no-one gets out of here alive'.

And it appeared Jim liked it that way; the 'green hotel' features in his poem *Celebration of the Lizard King* and he also shot a scene for his film *HWY* in Room 32. Some zealous fans believe that Jim is still hanging around, saying they have felt his presence and heard his mellifluous voice reverberating off the walls. But then people have been tapping into Jim's ghostly vibe wherever he laid his head, including his final resting place. Even journalists are keen to mistake a trick of the light at Père-Lachaise Cemetery in Paris (see page 109) for Morrison hovering above his own grave.

Still, Morrison was famous for relentlessly trying to 'break on through to the other side', so if he's going to put in a reappearance it may well be at one of his favourite old haunts.

Alta Cienega Motel, 1005 North La Cienega Boulevard, West Hollywood, CA 90069, USA

+1) 310 652 5797
manager@altacienega.com
www.altacienega.com

SEE

LAUREL CANYON

There has probably never been such a large concentration of musicians in one area, anywhere, as there once was in Laurel Canyon. In the 1960s, the area was heaving with rock stars. The rural canyon, tucked just behind Sunset, was home to Jim Morrison, who had a house just behind the County Store where Crosby, Stills and Nash met and began their country-rock ascent. Canned Heat had their studio up there while Frank Zappa had his log cabin. Marilyn Manson lived in the canyon for a while and recorded his 'Mechanical Animals' album in his pool house. Rick Rubin – the legendary record producer – has recorded notable acts such as Johnny Cash, Red Hot Chili Peppers, Slipknot, Slayer, System of a Down and Linkin Park at his Laurel Canyon studio, called 'The Mansion', which once belonged to Harry Houdini.

WHISKY A GO-GO

8901 Sunset Boulevard, West Hollywood, CA 90069;
www.whiskyagogo.com
Since throwing open its doors in 1964, Whisky a Go-Go has played host to myriad bands, including The Byrds, Janis Joplin and Led Zeppelin. The Doors were once the house band at this legendary club; and it helped to launch the careers of many a metal band, including Alice Cooper, Metallica and Guns N' Roses. Some may say that the Whisky is no longer the LA club at which to catch tomorrow's stars, but the club still puts on some great shows. It is

here that you'll catch guitar-slingers such as Slash jamming with other notable West-Hollywood residents.

BE SEEN

DUKES WEST HOLLYWOOD
8909 Sunset Boulevard, West Hollywood, CA 90069;
www.dukeswesthollywood.com
There is probably no other coffee shop on the planet with such rock 'n' roll credentials. This shop has served up brews for, among others, Jim Morrison, Janis Joplin, Tom Waits, The Runaways and Rickie Lee Jones. It may have relocated to its current address from its original home at the Tropicana Motel but this place remains synonymous with rock 'n' roll. Plus, it stays open well after all the clubs have closed.

RAINBOW BAR AND GRILL
9015 Sunset Boulevard, West Hollywood, CA 90069;
www.rainbowbarandgrill.com
This restaurant opened in 1972 with a party for Elton John, and quickly became a hangout for many rockers and their groupies. And John Belushi ate his last meal here (it was nothing flashy, by the way, just lentil soup). The Rainbow is still popular with local celebrities, including one Mr Lemmy Kilmister of Motörhead, and a great place for pre-gig drinks.

CHATEAU MARMONT

A night at the infamous Chateau Marmont, rising above the Sunset Strip like a leviathan of Gothic glamour, is part of the quintessential Hollywood experience. Actors, musicians, writers and the affluent elite – all have been known to hole themselves up in this legendary paparazzi-free zone in order to revel in romantic rebellion. Indeed, many guests even became habitués in order to trail a blaze with reckless abandon seven days a week.

Consequently, the tales from the Chateau have become so legendary that anyone with even a passing interest in rock 'n' roll, or any facet of the entertainment industry, for that matter, will have heard a Hollywood story related to Chateau Marmont. If you think you haven't, then maybe this list (by no means comprehensive) will jog your memory. James Dean hopped through a window to audition for *Rebel Without a Cause*; Judy Garland was known to have sung round the grand piano in the lobby; Canyon-cowboy Gram Parsons lived here for a short time; original Blues Brother John Belushi overdosed in bungalow 3; Led Zeppelin famously drove their Harley Davidsons into the hotel lobby; Jim Morrison dangled precariously from his window; esteemed record producer Rick Rubin lived here for 9 months after relocating from New York, so, during the 90s; John Frusciante, guitarist for the Red Hot Chili Peppers, took up residence here in 1996, only to descend into a drug hell (a descent so steep it nearly claimed the life of the young guitarist); Anthony Kiedis, also of the Red Hot Chili Peppers, recorded his vocals for 'By the Way' in his room; Ville Valo, vocalist for Finnish rockers HIM, recorded his vocals for the track 'Song or Suicide' here; Lindsay Lohan checked in following her arrest for drink driving in 2007; Lily Allen wrote the song 'Fuck You' while at the hotel; Heath Ledger partied here the week before he died. And now... take a breath.

As Harry Cohn, founder of Columbia Pictures, once succinctly said: 'If you must get in trouble, do it at the Chateau Marmont'. However, it should be noted that Frusciante was kicked out of the hotel when the extent of his drug-induced atrophy was revealed in the *New Times LA*.

So, what of the actual hotel? Well, despite being steeped in rock 'n' roll notoriety, it can actually offer much tranquillity. Modelled on a French castle in the Loire Valley, Chateau Marmont is at once luxe and unique. The pool area, which is accessed through a locked gate and tucked back from The Strip with lush vegetation, is serene and could certainly help you regain relative repose after a night of debauchery down on said Strip. The sumptuous lobby-lounge, too, is equally relaxing and as the sun lowers itself in the Californian sky casting long shadows across the dining patio, it's easy to just sink into a plush chair, savour the ambience and be seduced by the raffish glamour. However, that said, the Bar Marmont sign glimmers out on the street and, after you've sampled the Chateau's gastronomical delights, the bar is a great place to do some celeb-spotting.

Aside from the 63 rooms, the hotel also boasts garden cottages, hillside and poolside bungalows, and penthouses, all of which afford their guests total anonymity, if they so wish. So, tempting as it may be to run up to Val Kilmer and ask for an autograph, it is highly recommended that you don't – and we're speaking from experience here: sorry to have disturbed you, Scarlett. Owner André Balazs has even stated that he might throw someone out should they ask for an autograph, but to date, no one has ever been ejected from the premises for ything except not paying the bill (Warren Beatty and John usciante, reportedly) and for rubbing food over their face ritney Spears, allegedly).

Anyway, instead of ogling other celebrities for your entire ay, why not give in to your own inner rock-star and make use the 24-hour room service and in-room massage service? And, you really want to go Hollywood A-List, stay in Room 64, the o-bed penthouse (frequented by Howard Hughes so he could y on starlets down at the pool) complete with marble hallway d an enormous wrap-around terrace overlooking The Strip; it st so happens to be Bono's favourite room, too.

hateau Marmont, 8221 Sunset Boulevard, West ollywood, CA 90046, USA

1) 323 656 1010
servations@chateaumarmont.com
ww.chateaumarmont.com

SEE

LAUGH FACTORY
8001 Sunset Boulevard, West Hollywood, CA 90046;
www.laughfactory.com
The club's owner, Jamie Masada, established the Laugh Factory in Groucho Marx's old building at the tender age of 16 in 1979; he still comes into work almost every day. Comedy stars who have graced the stage here include Robin Williams, Jerry Seinfeld, Adam Sandler and Roseanne Barr. The Endurance Record was also broken here in January 2008 when Dane Cook delivered a set lasting more than seven hours.

KODAK THEATER
6801 Hollywood Boulevard, Hollywood, CA 90028;
www.kodaktheater.com
Experience Oscar night as the stars do: walk on the red carpet, glimpse an Oscar statuette and sit in the flip-down seats at the

ultimate awards venue – the Kodak Theater. Many of the world's top performers have sung, laughed and cried on its stage; musicians include Stevie Wonder, Prince, Alicia Keys and Tyler Perry. And with Grauman's Chinese Theater and Hollywood and Highland shopping complex just next door – the latter offering a great view of the Hollywood sign, incidentally – your Hollywood trip is complete.

BE SEEN

BARNEY'S BEANERY
8447 Santa Monica Boulevard, West Hollywood, CA 90069;
www.barneysbeanery.com
Described as 'a little bit of redneck' in an otherwise glamorous environment, Barney's is where Janis Joplin partied the night she overdosed. Loud, trashy and with plenty of greasy food (the menu features an incredible 150 burgers), this was once also a favourite hangout of Jim Morrison.

JONES HOLLYWOOD
7205 Santa Monica Boulevard, West Hollywood, CA 90046
A highly sociable and intimate environment awaits you at Jones', where you can enjoy the best apple pie in town and marvel at the red-and-black leather decor. There's an open-late kitchen, great music and celebrities just waiting to be spotted here; a night of fun and entertainment is guaranteed.

HIGHLAND GARDENS

The state of Texas can claim her as one of their own and the Rock and Roll Hall of Fame in Cleveland may be the proud keepers of her funky psychedelic Porsche, but it is the Highland Gardens in Hollywood that is home to Janis Joplin's spirit. Or the spirit of her age, at least.

Skirting the line between a voguish tranquil residential property and your all-American-style motel with a post and intel structure, the tired decor recalls an age when cool guys were 'cats', sexy women were 'foxy ladies' and this place was called The Landmark Hotel. That is to say, the abiding impression is one of a hotel irrevocably linked with the zeitgeist of 60s counterculture and consequently became a flophouse for groups and stars such as Jefferson Airplane and Janis Joplin. However, it was the latter who would forever be remembered as the hotel's most famous guest when she stayed in room 105 in October 1970 while working on the 'Pearl' record. Unfortunately, she would not get to complete the album. On October, after a particularly long day at the studio, Janis elected to unwind with a few screwdriver cocktails at rock-star haunt Barney's Beanery (see page 48). After leaving said watering hole she scored some heroin. However, it was not from her usual dealer, as he was out of town. The result was that she injected heroin that was 40 per cent pure as opposed to the usual street percentage of 1–2 per cent. The following day, October 1970, the Blues songstress was found dead, having overdosed on the heroin. The song she never got to put her whisky-soaked rasp to was the prophetically titled 'Buried Alive in the Blues'.

Joplin's entry into the 27 Club (27 is the cursed age at which many a rock star has expired; she was third that year, following the deaths of Jimi Hendrix and Canned Heat's Alan Wilson just a month earlier) secured her immortalisation. As a consequence of her tragic death, it is the brief stay of the groovy chanteuse that looms large over the hotel's history book. As a result, there are, of course, the obligatory ghost stories of Janis jangling her bangles in the middle of the night.

Highland Gardens Hotel, 7047 Franklin Avenue, Hollywood, CA 90028, USA

(+1) 323 850 0536
hghotel@aol.com
www.highlandgardenshotel.com

SEE

ESOTOURIC ROCK HISTORY TOUR
www.esotouric.com/rock
'Where The Action Was' is the name of Esotouric's rock 'n' roll history tour. If you don't fancy holing up at the Highland Gardens, then just view it from the tour bus. Travel back in time, starting from the 1960s, and visit all the notorious spots on Sunset Boulevard and around Hollywood. You won't just hear glittery tales of stardom, but of career highs and lows too – Phil Spector and Arthur Lee's, for instance – truly enlightening.

NEELY CUSTOM GUITARS
7424 Sunset Boulevard, West Hollywood, CA 90046;
www.neelyguitars.com
Directly across the street from Guitar Centre, experience the real thing at the home of the master of high-quality custom guitars – Dave Neely. Satisfied customers have included Bob Dylan, Tom Petty and Keith Richards. Got an annoying buzz? Problem with tension? Dave Neely will soon have your guitar sounding better than ever.

BE SEEN

THE TROUBADOUR

9081 Santa Monica Boulevard, West Hollywood, CA 90069;
www.troubadour.com

The place where Neil Diamond introduced Elton John to the stage, the 'troub' was once the Mecca for a burgeoning folk scene that included Joni Mitchell, the Eagles, Linda Ronstadt and, later, Tom Waits. It is also the venue that famously ejected John Lennon for drunkenly heckling folk duo The Smother Brothers after, bizarrely, taping a tampon to his own head. Aside from nursing his hangover the next day, Lennon also found time to send a bouquet of roses to Doug Weston – the Troubadour's then owner – by way of apology.

MUSSO & FRANK GRILL

6667 Hollywood Boulevard, Hollywood, CA 90028;
www.mussoandfrankgrill.com

In the same way the Highland Gardens is pitched between the putative glamour of the homes in the Hollywood Hills and the downtrodden who navigate the cracks on the boulevard of broken dreams, the Musso & Frank Grill, too, is a microcosm of Hollywood's celestial stars and lowly beings. This vintage bar has been serving troubadours and troubled transients since 1919. Many have pulled up a stool here, including Chandler and Chaplin, not to mention the most famous of barflies – Charles Bukowski. So, if you're looking for a strong drink that might imbue your pen with the Midas touch of LA's gritty writers, this is the place to come.

SUNSET MARQUIS

If the Terminator can become Governor of California then it's not incongruent to imagine a gym designed according to the whims of Keith Richards. This, after all, is Hollywood: exhilarating, histrionic and the place that all budding rock stars want to shine out against the neon bedlam of LA.

But beneath the flashy surface lies the quiet frustration of struggling actors, models and musicians, along with the sinking despair of those who were once the attention of Hollywood's fawning treatment but now find they've been expunged from the spotlight even quicker than they had entered it. But none of this is surprising, given that the city is built on the meritocratic idea that, here, you can be who you want to be. We can't all be rock stars, but we can sure-as-hell pretend. And, like the other hotels on Sunset Strip's rock 'n' roll road map, the Sunset Marquis recognises this enduring appeal, luring you in by peddling the promise of a rare glimpse into its orgy of luxury and glamour.

The fact that there is a 'paparazzi diversion' service underscores the view that the Sunset Marquis is indeed a sanctuary for many a celebrity. So, who's crashed and burned into the hotel's history books with their overzealousness? To list all the icons who've earned a place in the hotel's pantheon of debauchery would necessitate a coffee-table-sized book; in fact, the hotel has said that it may publish such a tome. In the meantime, whet your appetite with these few perennial tales that have helped define Sunset Marquis: a collective Red Hot Chili Peppers jumping from the roof; Tommy Lee and Pamela Anderson staging very public screaming matches; Depeche Mode vocalist David Gahan overdosing from a speedball; and Jeff Beck playing his guitar in the underground garage. But it's

Sunset Marquis

Courtney Love's ode 'Sunset Marquis' that captures the hotel's infernal heart best: 'Face down in front of the Sunset Marquis/You were the closest to God/We can do all the things that no-one believes'.

Inside this Mediterranean-style retreat the walls are adorned with signed photographs of rock's deities – taken on site by famous rock photographer Ross Halfin – confirming Sunset Marquis's unimpeachable title as *the* rock 'n' roll hotel. Of those grinning down on us, the likes of Ozzy Osbourne, Aerosmith, Slash, Billy Gibbons and Jeff Beck have all recorded at the hotel's plush NightBird recording studio – a state-of-the-art compound built in the wake of the aforementioned Jeff Beck's underground strumming. Legend has it that Jeff was picking his way through a few licks in his suite when the hotel's then manager, concerned about noise-levels, politely asked Jeff to rock-out beneath the hotel in the garage, so as to not disturb other guests. The said garage is now Studio A.

For post-session drinks, a roster of musicians can often be found cloistered together in Bar 1200 – a dimly lit laidback bar reserved for musicians and hotel guests. Or, if tranquillity is the order of the day, then perhaps you'll spot one or two in the serene garden, with its waterfall, koi ponds and tropical vegetation; certainly, this discreet oasis is where the hotel arcs beautifully between rock 'n' roll haven and Zen-like retreat.

Melding these two seemingly disparate notions further is the spa, which will see you kneaded to perfection while listening to soothing music on massage beds made by Porsche. Those looking to emulate the traditional rock-star stay should check into one of the villas. Reaffirming the hotel's rock 'n' roll mettle, amenities include 24-hour butler service, jacuzzis, use of the hotel's Bentley, private cabanas, not one but two heated outdoor pools, and villas with baby grand pianos. The suites – once tattered and torn from renegade living – no longer resemble seedy motel rooms; instead, they are light, airy and peppered with tints of mahogany and biscuit.

The mahogany hues continue throughout the restaurant, where the ambience is Californian cool and the cuisine Asian-French. The restaurant also has an outdoor terrace overlooking the calm of the gardens where you might just catch a glimpse of your favourite rocker sauntering over the pond's quaint little bridge. Given the relaxed atmosphere, away from the intrusive flashes of cameras, guests often find themselves at ease here. Suffice to say, it's easy to sit silently, take it all in and pretend you're the latest addition to LA's louche crowd.

Sunset Marquis, 1200 Alta Loma Road, West Hollywood, CA 90069, USA

(+1) 310 657 1333
reservations@sunsetmarquis.com
www.sunsetmarquis.com

SEE

GUITAR CENTER & ROCKWALK
7425 Sunset Boulevard, West Hollywood, CA 90046;
www.guitarcenter.com and www.rockwalk.com
The Guitar Center is a musical instrument superstore where you can buy or trade used and vintage gear. You can also dream and enter competitions to record your next release with Slash or play at Crossroads. What lies just outside the Guitar Center is just as special, however. The Rockwalk is a small patio with the handprints of rock stars from Chuck Berry to Alice Cooper.

GREYSTONE MANSION & PARK
905 Loma Vista Drive, Beverly Hills, CA 90210;
www.greystonemansion.org
For a touch of class, visit Greystone Park, where you can drive through the wrought-iron gates and marvel at the 55-room castle. Several Hollywood films were shot here, as was the video for

Meatloaf's 'I'd Do Anything for Love'. Directed by Michael Bay, the video took four days to film (Meatloaf's make-up took over two hours to apply) in temperatures upwards of 32°C.

BE SEEN

HOUSE OF BLUES
8430 Sunset Boulevard, West Hollywood, CA 90069;
www.houseofblues.com
Opened in 1994, this popular music venue has been decked out in the tin that was taken from the gin mill at the Delta Crossroads, where guitarist Robert Johnson allegedly made a pact with the devil (see page 73). Its ominous start has had a lasting effect: Frances Bean Cobain (daughter of Kurt Cobain and Courtney Love) celebrated her 16th birthday here with a suicide-themed bash. She went as her father, naturally.

THE ROXY THEATRE
9009 Sunset Boulevard, West Hollywood, CA 90069,
www.theroxyonsunset.com
The Roxy was opened in 1973 by famous music moguls Lou Adler and David Geffen. Since then it's had more than its fair share of memorable music moments from the likes of Guns N' Roses, Mötley Crüe, Nirvana and Bob Marley. It is also the venue at which John Belushi partied just hours before he died.

ANDAZ WEST HOLLYWOOD

I am a Golden God!' It is 1975, the height of rock music's heyday, and Robert Plant, Led Zeppelin's debonair vocalist, declares his rock-star status from his hotel room's balcony, overlooking the entertainment capital of the world.

Over the course of the mid-to-late 70s, Led Zeppelin and their entourage held court over as many as six floors at a time, from which TVs and bottles of Dom Pérignon were dropped from windows while motorcycles were driven down hallways. Such debauchery, however, was not confined to the likes of LedZep: a host of rock stars, including The Rolling Stones and The Who, wreaked havoc in what was once known as the 'Riot House'.

Thirty years later, and after a multimillion-dollar renovation, things are now a little different at this Hyatt hotel. For a start, the hotel has been rechristened for the fifth time. It was originally called the Gene Autry Hotel, upon opening in 1963, before becoming the Continental Hyatt House when it was sold on in 1966. Then, in 1976, it became the Hyatt on Sunset, only to be renamed again, in 1997, to the Hyatt West Hollywood, before eventually arriving at its current incarnation - Andaz West Hollywood.

Andaz, meaning 'personal touch' in Hindi, has worked its magic on the hotel as well as its service. The balconies of old have been enclosed in glass to create 'sun rooms', in which guests can enjoy city views but without the odd TV hurtling towards the boulevard below. As soon as you step beyond the glass facade, a congenial host will show you to the lounge (a sumptuous space defined by splashes of gold) and offer you a glass of wine before proceeding to check you in via a nifty handheld device that contains all your booking information; there's no impersonal front desk here.

If the check-in experience leaves you feeling like part of LA's well-heeled, then stepping into a Sunset Suite will give you the sensation of having just been sucked into the vortex of rock-star royalty. A spacious suite, incorporating a private dining area, living room and a marble bathroom, comes with all the trimmings: two flat-screen TVs, a small bar and wine refrigerator, plus a large teak balcony with a commanding view of the Hollywood Hills.

Deluxe Rooms boast views of the Sunset Strip as well as the skyline from Downtown out to the beaches. Plus, with floor-to-ceiling windows, there really is no obstructing your vista of a sprawling Los Angeles. Relax in a chaise longue in the sun room or cosy up on the loveseat sofa and enjoy the view.

The smallest type of room available, though no less alluring, is the Andaz King. Despite being a little more cosy, these smartly arranged rooms contain all the ingredients for a rock 'n' roll hotel: iHome stereo, huge flat-screen TV, black-out curtains, complimentary mini-bar (though it does feel somewhat incongruous to see it filled with non-alcoholic drinks) and a knock-out view of the Hollywood Hills.

The Andaz magic extends to the revamp of the old restaurant area; what used to be somewhat foreboding, swathed as it was in dark colours, now feels more inviting with its light-filled bar offering views of the revellers on Sunset. And it's easy to see why the restaurant RH (Riot House or Riot Hyatt, as the hotel was also known) often gets fully booked over the weekends; so if you want to sample its wares, better book ahead.

The anarchic antics of the 70s may have disappeared with the decadent decline of that decade, but the staff at the Andaz are keen to uphold the legacy of the Riot House days and wax nostalgically about those heady times. Though, if you wish to envisage the former glory days, watch Cameron Crowe's *Almost Famous*. The movie, filmed at the Andaz, regales the tales of 1970s excess, via the fictional story of a *Rolling Stones* journalist in hot pursuit of the ultimate interview with a rock band. In making the film the main floor of the Andaz was gutted and refurbished to look as it did back then. However, the hotel's days of attracting music's prime players are not lost to history as it continues to attract the hip new disciples, from Lindsay Lohan to Slipknot's Corey Taylor – the latter of whom was reportedly stopped from jumping from an eighth-floor balcony in 2003.

So, before hitting the clubs on Sunset, make your way to the rooftop deck for 'Pool Cocktail Hour' and seat yourself among the apex of an exclusive elite. Or failing that, just sample a cocktail and recall the end-of-tour party scene in *This is Spinal Tap*, which was filmed on this very rooftop.

Andaz West Hollywood, 8401 Sunset Boulevard, West Hollywood, CA 90069, USA

+1) 323 656 1234
www.westhollywood.hyatt.com

SEE

THE COMEDY STORE
8433 Sunset Boulevard, West Hollywood, CA 90069;
www.thecomedystore.com
Perhaps the most famous comedy venue in the world; this is also described as the darkest. Forget the rumours of hauntings by previous performers – it's just that they save the lights for the stages. All the greats, from Richard Pryor to Robin Williams to Jim Carrey, have performed here.

MELROSE AVENUE
West Hollywood
Located along The Strip between Fairfax and Poinsettia, Melrose Avenue once attracted crowds of punk and rock poseurs. Although

the vintage and alt-rock clothing and records shops have now been joined by the regular coffee houses, you'll still find a good selection of gear there. Just don't expect any of the shops to be open before noon.

BE SEEN

CAFÉ LA BOHÈME
8400 Santa Monica Boulevard, West Hollywood, CA 90069; see www.globaldiningca.com

Treat yourself to cuisine Californian style (influenced by Asian and European flavours) at this seductive bistro. For less formal affairs, try the bar menu in the intimate lounge. With rock-star booths upstairs, chandeliers and wood-burning fireplaces, this is the perfect place to get to know that special someone.

THE VIPER ROOM
8852 Sunset Boulevard, West Hollywood, CA 90069; www.viperroom.com

Partly owned by Johnny Depp until 2004, this music venue is famous for being the location at which River Phoenix died in 1993. It still hosts up-and-coming bands. Over the years the club has been a hangout for Sean Penn, Jennifer Aniston and Adam Duritz, vocalist for Counting Crows. The club also features in the documentary *Dig!* as the venue at which the notorious The Brian Jonestown Massacre group scupper all chances of a record deal when their show ends prematurely due to interband brawling.

THE JOSHUA TREE INN

—◦✕✦✕◦—

Just three hours' drive from the sprawling seismic entertainment factories of LA, arid winds from the desiccated Californian desert send detritus swirling round a hacienda-style settlement called the Joshua Tree Inn. Teetering on the empty expanse of a dust bowl that has attracted visitors with its apocryphal stories of UFOs, the U-shaped hotel, with its weathered verandas seemingly tethered by desert vine, has all the hallmarks of an outpost for outlaws; or, when dusk looms, it is reminiscent of a haunted house. Indeed, there is a strange 'worldliness' about the Joshua Tree Inn, which evokes a mood of primeval mysticism that causes a brief spine-chill.

Standing on a wild primitive landscape, the Joshua Tree offered an escape for rock stars from the pressures of LA's scrutinising glare: Keith Richards was known to stumble across the desert courtyard banjaxed on coke, while pseudo desperados The Eagles and hardcore troubadour Steve Earle are also among those who have been lured to the solitary plains specked with cacti and wild flowers. However, in addition to those who have been drawn to the Joshua Tree by tales of weird lights in the sky, the hotel has, in the main, lured pilgrims whose interest has been piqued by the tale of Gram Parsons.

On 18 September 1973, Gram – the Laurel Canyon cowboy who often fled to the desert for respite – checked into the Joshua Tree Inn for the last time. Ensconced in Room 8, Gram overdosed on a heroin-and-cocaine speedball. Seeing Gram's lips turn a deathly shade, two friends, who had accompanied Gram on this particular fateful excursion, tried to rouse the unconscious singer with mouth-to-mouth resuscitation and, in desperation, even resorted to the old revival trick of inserting ice cubes into the anus, in an attempt to keep him from slipping away. Despite a momentary flicker of hope, Gram was pronounced dead just hours later on the morning of 19 September.

Remarkably, the wistful tale doesn't end there: remembering a promise he made to Gram at a funeral just months earlier, road manager and close friend Phil Kaufman knew he had to honour Gram's wish to be cremated out in the desert. But upholding such a promise was not without its problems. By 21 September, Gram's body was already at the airport, on its way to Louisiana, at the request of his stepfather. This situation precipitated a body-snatch-coup that saw Kaufman borrowing a hearse, stealing the body and driving it back out to Joshua Tree to watch it burn under the desert's star-filled sky.

The circumstances surrounding Gram's death no doubt mean he is irrevocably associated with the Joshua Tree Inn; moreover, the hotel has since become something of a guardian of the country rock star's legacy. Open the door of Room 8 (now called the Gram Parsons Room) and it's like stepping back into 1973; the room has retained the mirror and picture that hung on the peach-coloured walls during Gram's stay. There is also a guestbook for fans to record their tributes. Among the entries is a touching eulogy from Gram's daughter, Polly Parsons, who sometimes stays in the room herself.

The morbid appeal of sleeping in the room where a troubled troubadour ended his days may be the hotel's only cachet for some visitors. Certainly, the hotel is denuded of five-star luxury – there's not even high-speed Internet, let alone a butler service – but that's not what this hotel is about. Apart from the obvious romantic rock 'n' roll myths, people come here for very much the same reason Keith Richards and Gram Parsons came: to sit beneath a captivating starlit sky, far from the drudgery of a modern existence that filches something from our spirituality. But that's not to say that the hotel is without beauty; the charm lies in the hotel's vestigial character. The rustic stone fireplace that greets you in the living room guarantees a cosy evening gazing upon the embers with a glass of wine while the whole hotel is surrounded by the unbridled beauty of the wilderness.

Mercifully avoiding the temptation to turn the entire hotel into a shrine for Gram Parsons, the Joshua Tree Inn has fashioned each room according to its own distinct style and comes with a smattering of modern amenities: refrigerator, microwave and cable TV. Nonetheless, if you're the sort of person to complain about a grouting issue in the bathroom, then best for your blood pressure to stay somewhere else; after all, this is not Chateau Marmont. Yet, despite the lack of amenities to accommodate rock megalomania, this hotel is the barnacle that has fastened Joshua Tree to rock 'n' roll legend, alongside the equally rustic Rancho de la Luna – the famous recording studios at which Josh Homme conducts his collaborative desert jamming sessions.

The Joshua Tree Inn's kudos isn't confined to Room 8, however. Donovan – another plaintive singer-songwriter – also has a room named after him. The Donovan Suite is ideal for families as it includes a king-sized bed, two beds in the living room, a full kitchen and a private patio area. And, unlike poor Gram, Donovan is still a regular guest of the hotel and often stays in his 'own' room. Although, having said that, there are those who believe Room 8 to be haunted with Gram's spirit, so perhaps Gram still uses his own room too; who knows?

The Joshua Tree Inn, 61259 29 Palms Highway, Joshua Tree, CA 92252, USA

(+1) 760 366 1188
joshuatreeinn@gmail.com
www.joshuatreeinn.com

SEE

JOSHUA TREE PARK
www.nps.gov/jotr
If you fancy some off-road action or just a change of scenery, head for what local rock-climbers call 'JT'. The park is a haven for climbers, scramblers, hikers, campers and off-road drivers. Covering an area of almost 800,000 acres, it includes parts of the higher and cooler Mojave (home to the *Yucca brevifolia* or Joshua Tree) and lower Colorado deserts.

YUCCA VALLEY
If the quiet gets a bit much, and you and your friends or family get bored of recreating the album cover shoot of U2's 'The Joshua Tree' in the desert, head into Yucca Valley: the nearest town outside Joshua Tree that offers more in the way of restaurants, shopping and welcome diversion.

BE SEEN

JOSHUA TREE MUSIC FESTIVAL
www.joshuatreemusicfestival.com
A municipal event with an eclectic line-up, this festival is a chilled way to integrate yourself into a dusty-town community via music and art. Those into the alt-country rock of Gram and the folk peddled by Donovan, in particular, will enjoy this biannual event, held in May and October; with the former date taking in everything from reggae to hip-hop beats, while the latter date is more roots-focussed.

PAPPY AND HARRIET'S
53688 Pioneertown Road, Pioneertown, CA 92268;
www.pappyandharriets.com
Built as part of a Western stage set in the 1940s, Pappy and Harriet's boasts live music four nights a week and lies just a 15-minute drive away from the Joshua Tree Inn. Lucinda Williams, Shelby Lynne and Michelle Shocked have all played here. It's much more than just a venue for music, though, and offers a wide range of Tex-Mex, grills, salads and sandwiches five days a week (closed Tuesdays and Wednesdays).

HARD ROCK LAS VEGAS

His position as 'the world's greatest bass player' (he was known as Thunderfingers, after all) in one of 'the world's greatest rock bands' is perhaps at odds with his once humble aspirations to run a pub with Queenie – his dear old mum. On the other hand, you could cite such an ambition as simply being in keeping with his modest beginnings in Ealing, West London: a place where he would strum an electric guitar, *sans* amplifier, in the living room above Queenie's pub while she darned his socks. Inevitably, however, it would be a dream doomed to remain elusive as it wasn't long before the bassist climbed aboard the rock 'n' roll juggernaut. Who is this bassist? The Who's John Entwistle.

Having been put through the rock 'n' roll wringer with drugs, gambling and lascivious women, Entwistle was facing the precipice of bankruptcy by the time the noughties swung round. And so, fearing a financial abyss, he managed to inveigle the rest of The Who into hitting the road in 2002.

Holed up in the Hard Rock Hotel in Sin City, Entwistle was at the full mercy of his libidinous urges. An evening here was obviously not going to be without its wantonness and, within his role as rock star, perhaps Thunderfingers considered his reckless living as merely acting decorously. The only problem was that years of abuse had lambasted his coronary arteries and his blood pressure had soared higher than a Pete Townshend stage leap. 'I hope I die before I get old' rang truer than ever to these veteran rockers, who would not even get to play the first scheduled show. On 27 June 2002, just one day before the tour was due to kick off, John Entwistle was found dead at 10a.m., allegedly, by the stripper he had spent the previous evening with. Cause of death: cocaine-induced heart attack.

Out of respect for the bassist, the hotel management elected not to dub the room in which Thunderfingers cashed in his (casino) chips 'The John Entwistle Room'. While this may cause a bit of grousing among the diehard fans eager to get as close as they can, furrowed brows will soon be smoothed upon discovering the dedication this hotel pays to the glory of rock 'n' roll as a whole. First, there's the stupefying amount of iconic memorabilia: Keith Richard's guitar, motorbikes that once belonged to Mötley Crüe's Nikki Sixx and Guns N' Roses' Matt Sorum, Prince's 'Purple Rain' suit, the Aerosmith leather jackets and Madonna's underwear… the list goes on, but it'll probably be more fun for you if you stumble across an artefact unexpectedly.

If the rock 'n' roll paraphernalia has whetted your appetite then just wait until you see the hotel's pool areas during the poolside party that is Rehab: a bacchanal of scantily clad women breeze through tropical trees to dip into a pool already brimming with the bronzed and beautiful. Beyond the hoopla poolside, the party continues unabated inside. The hotel's music venue – the Joint – frequently has its walls rattled by the classic and the contemporary: from The Rolling Stones to The Black Crowes, and from Santana to Foo Fighters, many have roused this rock club, which manages to galvanise gig-goers with the prospect of skyboxes and VIP seating.

And the rock 'n' roll doesn't end there. The Penthouse Suite will keep the delirious thrills coming with its private bowling alley and hot tub that overlooks The Strip. A view of The Strip is also the draw of the Deluxe Suites, though the madness of the gambling dominion below can't be surveyed from the vantage point of a hot tub. If, however, your stay is not being funded by your very own Peter Grant, you may opt for a room in the

Paradise Tower. While the rooms don't speak of the same opulence, they're still plugged into the rock 'n' roll spirit. Dimly lit and with sleek dark furnishings exuding a subtle Gothic aura, these rooms lend themselves decadently to a night of orgiastic pleasure. Ultimately, whichever room you plunge for, you're marking yourself out as one who loves nothing more than a bit of riotous fun.

A criticism often levelled at Las Vegas is that it is unashamedly artificial; a place with no authentic history of its own, it has filched landmarks from the history books and ended up placing fake pyramids next to its strip clubs. But it's this playful approach that makes Vegas hotels, such as this one, places of such misadventure. Where else could you take a swim in a pool that plays rock music underwater, watch Go-Go dancers while playing blackjack, catch a high-profile gig and then finish the night off in a rock club, all without leaving the hotel?

Hard Rock Hotel & Casino, 4455 Paradise Road, Las Vegas, NV 89169, USA

+1) 702 693 5000
www.hardrockhotel.com

SEE

BELLAGIO FOUNTAINS
3600 Las Vegas Boulevard South, Las Vegas, NV 89109;
www.bellagio.com
Immortalised in film, the Bellagio fountain show continues to attract tourists to its choreographed water spectacle. No doubt, you will have seen snippets of the display in numerous movies, but to be present at one of the actual nightly showings is something else as it forces your gaze to follow its ascent high into the Vegas sky. Slightly more impressive than watching it at just a few inches high

on your TV. The shows take place every half-hour between 3p.m. and 8p.m., and every 15 minutes from then until midnight.

GRAND CANYON

If you feel like you've been holed up in a glitterball in the middle of the desert for too long, take the 180-mile trip to see the natural marvels of the Grand Canyon. Helicopter trips tend to go to the west rim, where you can also do the skywalk (the short but spectacular semi-circular walk over the gorge while looking down 1,200 metres (4,000 feet) through the glass floor).

BE SEEN

THE JOINT

Hard Rock Hotel & Casino; www.hardrockhotel.com

The Joint is now twice as large as it used to be but it hasn't lost any of its original rock credence gained from hosting greats such as The Rolling Stones, Bob Bylan, David Bowie and Aerosmith. Let the super-tall speaker bays (think taller than a two-storey house!) blast your ears as you marvel at the many plasma screens. Make yourself comfortable in the VIP lounge or sweat it out on the dancefloor.

DOUBLE DOWN SALOON

4640 Paradise Road, Las Vegas, NV 89169;
www.doubledownsaloon.com

Describing itself as the 'anti-Vegas', the Double Down is the place to head here when you want to pretend you're no longer in Vegas. With live music, pinball, pool, hallucinogenic graffiti, tatty sofas and the most amazing jukebox, this place has been bringing 'much-needed sophistication' to Vegas since 1992. The doors never close and all the shows, including live punk and alt-rock music, are free.

HARD ROCK SAN DIEGO

When rock 'n' roll's last axe-slinging hero, Slash, teamed up with the Black Eyed Peas' pop 'Dutchess' Fergie, for his eponymously titled album, many a rock music elitist snorted incredulously at the news. Then they heard Fergie's fiery vocals on the storming collaborative track 'Beautiful Dangerous' and were consequently blown away. Those who were caught off guard upon hearing the aforementioned song may do well to remember that moment when checking into the Black Eyed Peas Rock Star Suite at San Diego's Hard Rock Hotel, if only to brace themselves for being bowled over once again.

You see, while the Black Eyed Peas may operate, primarily, within the hip-hop/pop paradigm, they also seem to know a thing or two when it comes to rocking out with the fraternity. The namesake suite, custom-designed by the Grammy-award-winning act, not only bears their inimitable imprint (there's plenty of the group's signed memorabilia on display) but also has enough of an edgy vibe to make it a veritable rock 'n' roll roost. As you enter the suite, you're greeted by a video of will.i.am, who recommends a few places to visit in the famed Gaslamp Quarter, before you're able to feast your eyes on a living room big enough to host your own celeb party. This luxury suite also boasts an oversized and well-stocked mini bar, and has a spacious square patio, with the best view of Woodstock Terrace – the outdoor event space that has had performers such as Dave Navarro and the Goo Goo Dolls tread its boards. Suffice to say, it's a swish playpen that matches the sense of drama witnessed at the suite's inaugural opening celebrations, for which Fergie sidestepped the customary ribbon-cutting scenario in favour of taking a chainsaw –

encrusted with 7488 rhinestones, no less – to the Grand Opening sign, before joining the rest of her band for a rooftop gig.

Of course, as you'd expect from this franchise, the rock-star glitz is not confined to one suite. There are 17 loft-style Rock Star Suites; each exuding exemplary rock-star living, albeit with differentiating colour themes and styles. Aside from the Black Eyed Peas' party pad, the Diamond Suite will see the dukes of rock vying for the luminous throne – read halo-illuminated king beds that come with 'Sleep Like a Rock' bedding. However, no doubt, the huge HD flat screens and private outdoor jacuzzi will ensure you get to relax in true rock-star style.

So, you're ensconced within the walls of a rocker's haunt, but do you look the part? If not, head down to the hotel's Rock Shop where you can kit yourself out in all the requisite regalia, including T-shirts designed exclusively by Ozzy Osbourne, Bruce Springsteen and Green Day. Now, you're there and you've got the T-shirt, but if you're still not feeling the rock-star vibe, then maybe a Harley Davidson would accentuate your (priapic) star qualities? If this is the sort of look you're after then book The Hard Rock and a Hog Package, which includes: two nights accommodation, day rental from San Diego Harley Davidson, a detailed map of the best hog rides in the San Diego area, a gift bag of Harley Davidson goodies and $40 meal credit for an early morning breakfast at Maryjane's (though, to be honest, you'll probably miss breakfast because the package also includes VIP access to two of the hotel's nightclubs, Float and 207).

Once you've donned your new rock-star finery, returned from the open road (*Easy-Rider*-style), tasted the delights of Japanese cuisine at Nobu restaurant and taken your place at the black-leather bar with a few cocktails in 207, a perfect night's

leep will no doubt follow, aided by a playlist of chilled music
reated by the hotel's 'vibe manager' as part of its turn-down
ervice.

As you've probably surmised, this superlative hotel is
vidently a place where the rich and famous can get pampered
nd partied out. But the Black Eyed Peas are also making sure
ome of their money leaves the hotel: money made from their
uite benefits the group's Peapod foundation – a charity that
elps provide opportunities to children worldwide. And if
noney is ever made from the sale of the suite, all proceeds will
o to the charity. Please note: rhinestone chainsaw not included.

lard Rock Hotel San Diego, 207 5th Avenue, San Diego,
A 92101, USA

1) 619 702 3000
ww.hardrockhotelsd.com

SEE

ROCK 'N' ROLL MARATHON
San Diego; runrocknroll.competitor.com
Past years have seen Elvis in the marathon – not the King himself, of
course, but a plethora of Elvis-impersonating runners. This annual
June event has over 40 bands playing live music in the streets lining
the race route, and after all that exertion there's a huge concert and
after-run party.

TUMCO – CALIFORNIAN GHOST TOWN
If you've had your fill of the hustle and bustle of the city, then head
out of town on Route 8 to the ghost town of Tumco (The Union
Mining Company). A 19th-century gold-mining town with saloons
and a red-light district, Tumco has a high grave-count at its
cemetery. Take a walking ghost tour – just be careful where you
tread, you don't want to fall down an abandoned mine shaft.

BE SEEN

THE CASBAH
2501 Kettner Boulevard, San Diego, CA 92101;
www.casbahmusic.com
Opening at the tail end of the 1980s with a capacity of just 75, the Casbah has since moved to a new plush location to welcome up to 200 revellers. Many bands have entertained in this intimate venue, including The White Stripes, Basement Jaxx, Weezer and The Damned. This alternative music venue has sofas and alcoves and, if that's not enough, also features pool tables, pinball and the classic video game Galaga.

WINSTON'S
1921 Bacon Street, San Diego, CA 92107; www.winstonsob.com
Aside from the live music, this beach club is also known to host comedy and spoken word poetry, and showcases local art. Oh, and Electric Waste Band – one of America's top Grateful Dead tribute bands – put in regular appearances. Time your visit wisely.

SHERATON GUNTER

Long before Black Sabbath struck the devil's note, simultaneously creating heavy metal and pricking the ears of Lucifer, his infernal majesty had a predilection for the plaintive blues. His horned ears were piqued when a promising guitarist from the Mississippi summoned him to the crossroads to make a Faustian pact. The agreement was that Lucifer would gain the young man's soul in exchange for bestowing upon him exemplary guitar-playing abilities. It is a tale long entrenched in music folklore by the speedy transition from rudimentary to awe-inspiring skills of that young Mississippi guitarist. His name was Robert Johnson and it is a myth that he did nothing to dispel in his song 'Cross Road Blues'.

Regardless of how Johnson attained his mastery of the blues, the one facet of the Robert Johnson legend on which guitar connoisseurs – including Eric Clapton, Jeff Beck, Bob Dylan and Muddy Waters – are unequivocal is that the young outsider vanished from the Mississippi only to return with a repertoire of songs that would eventually have him branded as the King of Blues.

Having been brought to the attention of Vocalion Records, Johnson was invited to record his lonesome blues by the label's producer, Don Law, in Rooms 413 and 414 of the Gunter Hotel, where a temporary studio had been set up, on 3 November 1936. A shy drifter who was evidently nervous in the unfamiliar setting of a studio, Johnson only settled into the songs once the recording engineers had retreated behind the glass to the control room. Then, hunched over his guitar, Johnson turned his back, sang into a corner of the room, close to to the mic, very much self-contained, and unleashed a spectral voice that chilled the spine, over some guitar licks that are now heralded as some of the finest riffs ever written.

The recording sessions were not without their problems, however. After the first day of recording, in which Johnson incredibly recorded eight tracks, Law received a phone call: Johnson had wound up in jail. Upon returning to the hotel to resume recording, Johnson managed to cut only one more track. He returned for that final day of recording on 27 November – the session at which he captured the infamous 'Cross Road Blues'.

But it would seem that a conduit between Johnson and the devil was agape and that Old Nick was only too eager to call upon the young Delta Blues singer to pay his dues. And so it goes that, in August 1938, Johnson was fatally poisoned by the jealous husband of a woman who he was trying to impress. With such a short tenure as a recording artist, the modicum of success Johnson had was all too fleeting, leaving him relatively unknown in his lifetime. His inevitable assailment into rock 'n' roll consciousness came posthumously, when the likes of Cream, The Doors, Led Zeppelin and The Rolling Stones covered his songs.

In view of the dearth of Robert Johnson mementos in the archive (just two confirmed photos of Johnson exist) it's perhaps not surprising to learn that Rooms 413 and 414 don't come adorned with Johnson relics. But that doesn't stop people wanting to visit said rooms. Grammy-award-winning rocker John Mellencamp made a pilgrimage to the room to record a track there, in the hope of imbuing the song with some of that desolate Delta Blues spirit that Johnson so perfectly encapsulated.

It's to the hotel's credit that they haven't decorated the room with mock memorabilia in order to milk the cash cow. Instead, like the other guest rooms, Room 414 is genially urnished in shades of burnt sienna and biscuit with dashes of deep red, soft white and blues. Take into account the hotel's own Sheraton Sweet Sleeper Pillow-top Bed and you can't imagine anyone or anything disturbing your sleep.

As well as a great night's sleep, the Gunter also promises some of the best-tasting food around. The most notable is at the award-winning Sheraton Gunter Bakery, which opened at the same time as the hotel, over 100 years ago; as well as its freshly baked goods, there are the to-die-for strawberries and chocolate. For a more sophisticated dining experience, head to Barron's Restaurant for its excellent Grilled Salmon and Petit Beef Tenderloin, or if you fancy a drink and a slouch in a sofa then McLeod's Pub is informal, comfortable and relaxed, with some of the decor resembling that of a traditional British pub.

For all its elegance, exquisite dining and comfortable rooms, it is the legend of Robert Johnson that looms large at the Gunter Hotel. The Mississippi-born vagabond has certainly inspired many a great band. Couple myth with talent and you'll always have the ingredients for the archetypal rock star. He also proves that the devil really did always have the best tunes.

Sheraton Gunter Hotel, 205 East Houston Street, San Antonio, TX 78205, USA

+1) 210 227 3241
reservations@gunterhotel.com
www.gunterhotel.com

SEE

THE ALAMO

300 Alamo Plaza, San Antonio, TX 78205; www.thealamo.org
The most famous San Antonio mission, the Alamo (originally called San Antonio de Valero) was built for colonial expansion by the Spanish in the early 18th century. In February 1836, Mexican troops reclaimed the Alamo and executed the majority of those fighting to defend it. It is also known for being the place where Ozzy Osbourne once took a piss while wearing his wife's dress.

RIVER WALK

www.thesanantonioriverwalk.com
Stroll along this delightful network of walkways along the banks of the San Antonio River, lined with shops, bars, restaurants and attractions such as the San Antonio Museum of Art and the Pearl Brewery. If this all sounds too civilised, drop by in January when the river is drained for the annual Mud Festival, which includes a Mud Art Festival and Mud King and Queen Coronation.

BE SEEN

JOHN T. FLOORE'S COUNTRY STORE

14492 Old Bandera Road, Helotes, TX 78023;
www.liveatfloores.com
Proving that sometimes the old ones really are the best ones, this venue has been supporting live music since its inception in 1946. Since then, the likes of Elvis, BB King and Johnny Cash have trodden the boards, making it a veritable addition to Texas' music history. With a barbeque almost every night, Floore's is a must-go-to place. Get there early as the bar gets busy regardless of the time of year.

HOWL AT THE MOON

111 West Crockett Street, San Antonio, TX 78205;
www.howlatthemoon.com
If you feel the urge to sing, visit Howl at the Moon for a rock 'n' roll duelling piano show. It's a great place for drunken silliness; you can't help but have fun here.

ST PETER HOUSE

Johnny Thunders' life ended in very much the same way it started: in the fetal position. He was found curled up under the coffee table in his hotel room (it was Room 37, in case you're curious), drugs finally having won the narcotic onslaught that had consumed the thorny-haired guitarist since his days in the New York Dolls. By the time Thunders had been found, incipient rigor mortis had set in, which meant that a very stiff and U-shaped Johnny had to check out of his room in a body bag. For the New Orleans police this was just another junkie whose perilous taste for drugs was his undoing.

Friends and family of Thunders, however, believe that further investigation into Johnny's death is still warranted. For a start, Johnny's passport and clothes had been pilfered, which does some way to suggesting that foul play may have played a part in this rock star's final descent. This anomaly was compounded by the coroner's report, which revealed that the drug dosage administered to Thunders was not a fatal one. But nothing was clear-cut with Thunders' decline; there was no way of telling just when or how he would shuffle off this mortal coil. The fact that the autopsy revealed Thunders to also be in the throes of advanced leukaemia just goes to show the multiplicity of his problems.

The New York guitarist had decamped to New Orleans in order to make a final bid for the rock-star stratosphere, which had so far eluded him. But the fact that Thunders was unable to surmount the type of success Keith Richards (the archetypal rock 'n' roller on which Thunders modelled his own barbed coiffure and drunken stagger) was able to enjoy, was no surprise. Thunders' career had been dogged by drugs and bad decisions:

he was already puking behind his amp with his first group, the New York Dolls, before taking his sophomore act, The Heartbreakers, out on the poorly attended Anarchy Tour with the Sex Pistols in late 1976. He later performed as a solo artist but, by this point, his autonomy had been obliterated by heroin. So, taken with the city's jazz heritage as he was, New Orleans was intended to be the new start for our anti-hero, only for it to end up as… well, the end.

As with most rock 'n' roll deaths, rumours abound when it comes to the circumstances under which Thunders made his exit. Adding another shadowy strand to the already dark tale is the story of how, once Thunders had rolled into New Orleans in April 1991, his antennae for destruction immediately picked up on two addicts in a bar. The three of them shuffled off to St Peter House Hotel where, under the junkie tutelage of these two fiends, Thunders allegedly took a lethal hit of narcotics.

If rock-star kudos can be marked by the luxury status of the hotels musicians frequent, then Johnny Thunders' ranking as underground legend, rather than jet-owning arena-rocking icon, is hard to refute. While St Peter's is far from being the damp cesspool checked into by bands who share a bed, a van, and a pizza for lunch, it's also far from being the MGM Grand. Come to St Peter's for freshly baked pastries enjoyed out on the balcony in the morning sun, not to throw a TV from a sumptuous penthouse's window. It can be found tucked away in the French Quarter – the oldest part of town – with traces of that old New Orleans world charm abounding, from the pink frontage wrapped in an iron-lace balcony, to the two quaint courtyards overlooked by some of the rooms. Each guest room appointed differently but all speak of the same charm and are adorned with antique furnishings. Some of the rooms have canopy beds and share the wrap-around balcony too.

Having survived Hurricane Katrina (not to mention a couple of fires too) you could say that this 200-year-old hotel has done pretty well to continue standing in its original guise. To that end, the hotel really fits in with the rest of the neighbourhood, maintaining that distinctive New Orleans flavour, making it one of a kind. The real coup for this hotel though (apart from offering the room in which our gutter-punk expired) is its location. The famous Bourbon Street is just two blocks away and features such famous bars as The Cat's Meow and The Famous Door, as well as the famous strip club Larry Flynt's Barely Legal Club.

And, of course, no rock 'n' roll death would be complete without the obligatory ghost story. Many guests have, allegedly, heard the burnt-out Thunders banging about the room. No reports of hearing voices, though, which can only be a good thing. If we couldn't fathom his requisite slur in life, what hope have we of deciphering his slurred punk sneer when it's coming from the other side?

St Peter House Hotel, 1005 Saint Peter Street, New Orleans, LA 70116, USA

(1) 800 535 7815
www.stpeterhouse.com

SEE

YE OLDE ORIGINAL DUNGEON
738 Toulouse Street, French Quarter, New Orleans, LA 70130;
www.originaldungeon.com
In a town famous for voodoo, drinking and the motto *'Laissez les bons temps rouler'* (or 'let the good times roll'), it's not surprising that a venue like Ye Olde Original Dungeon exists in New Orleans. It's Halloween year-round in this spooky club where the lights burn red, tables are set within jail cells and the rock music is cranked to the max. Designed for creatures of the night, it doesn't open until midnight, by which time you'll be able to sample their signature drinks – Witch's Brew and Dragon's Blood.

HAUNTED HISTORY TOUR
723 St Peter Street, New Orleans, LA 70119;
www.hauntedhistorytours.com
If the dark and sinister past of the St Peter House Hotel leaves you wanting more, explore the rest of the French Quarter with a guided ghost tour. Visit the tomb of Voodoo Queen Marie Laveau in the city's oldest burial ground and the sites of documented hauntings along Vieux Carre.

BE SEEN

TIPITINA'S
501 Napoleon Avenue, New Orleans, LA 70115; www.tipitinas.com
Taking its name from one of Professor Longhair's hits, this legendary venue has hosted home-grown luminaries such as The Neville Brothers and The Meters as well as international acts such as Nine Inch Nails, Pearl Jam and Lenny Kravitz. The two-storey club now houses a recording studio and a record label and continues to run an impressive gig calendar.

FRENCH QUARTER FESTIVAL
www.fqfi.org
The largest free music celebration in the world, the French Quarter Festival is held every April. Eighteen stages throughout the French Quarter host the best in local jazz, funk, rhythm and blues, and world music.

HEARTBREAK HOTEL

~─❦❦❦─~

Whether you're sporting a quiffed coiffure as an impersonator working in faithful tribute to the King, or merely lampooning the bloated burger-chomping image of his later years at a fancy dress party, few can deny the cultural and musical impact this hip-swinger had on the world. A protégé from Sam Phillips' stable of budding stars, Presley was a force of personality who brought some *joie de vivre* to an otherwise staid era. Granted, the groundwork may have been laid by other artists, but the arrival of Elvis meant the fuse was well and truly lit for the emergence of rock 'n' roll as a lifestyle.

Fittingly, then, Heartbreak Hotel is well versed in the sprightly style closely associated with Presley. Flaunting his vivacious flair from the off, the hotel's lobby is ablaze with retina-scorching colours of bright red, purple and blue, topped off with a scattering of faux animal prints. In keeping with the unswervingly retro feel so zealously bestowed upon guests at check-in, the four Elvis-themed suites have been artfully arranged in the same gung-ho fashion.

The Graceland Suite is undoubtedly the most celebrated suite given that it is an imitation Graceland Mansion in diminutive form. Aside from mirroring the kitsch decor with which Presley, and his actress girlfriend, festooned their own 14-acre Graceland home, the suite comes complete with replica 'billiard room' and 'jungle room'. To see the genuine articles, just cross over the road to the venerated Graceland estate, still standing in all its white-columned glory.

The Gold & Platinum Suite, meanwhile, sparkles with more glitz than the sequins on Elvis's lamé stage gear. Central to this primped suite is a large Elvis record that serves as a table –

a forthright nod to his success as a recording artist – while the sand-coloured wood floors complement a room bespangled wit silver furnishings and mirrored ceiling.

The homage is continued in the art deco Hollywood Suite where tribute is paid to Presley's cinematic triumphs. Again, nothing is tame: rugs are patterned with diamond shapes of black and leopard-skin and the carpets are deep crimson; but your attention will no doubt be quickly diverted away from the dizzying decor as you notice that the suite boasts its own privat bar and cinema.

If your tongue is firmly in cheek, then plump for the deepl romantic Burning Love Suite. Yup, you've guessed it: another suite that is openly gaudy, this time by dint of the gold and pin upholstery. While all of the rooms are good fun, you'll probably need to be somewhat of an ardent Elvis fan to make full use of the 24-hour Elvis movie channel. But should you tire of watching the famous gyrator swing his hips and curl his lip, relax on a chaise longue by the heart-shaped pool or take some time out in the Jungle Room Lounge.

If you can't decide which suite you would like to reserve, you can mix-and-match, whereby you book one of the suite's bedrooms and request an adjoining room belonging to another themed-suite, allowing you enough space to sleep up to eight people (depending on how big your entourage is). If you're looking for something that's a bit easier on the eye, then the regular guest rooms tend to limit their ostentation to diamond-patterned bedspreads and hues of royal blue and gold

Ultimately, if you're choosing to stay here, you'll no doubt be in pursuit of the whole Elvis experience. To get the complet Elvis exposé, check the hotel's website for package deals as the often tie in excursions that will satisfy any Elvis enthusiast.

With this in mind, is it any wonder there is a 'laughing version' of 'Are You Lonesome Tonight?'? Incidentally, if you've not heard the famous Vegas performance in which Presley loses himself in fits of giggles, seek it out: the track will serve as a great mood-setter for your stay here, as this class of rock 'n' roll hotel embodies the same playful sense of humour.

Heartbreak Hotel, 3677 Elvis Presley Boulevard, Memphis, TN 38116, USA

(+1) 901 332 1000
heartbreakhotel@elvis.com
www.elvis.com/epheartbreakhotel

SEE

SUN STUDIO
706 Union Avenue, Memphis, TN 38103; www.sunstudio.com
Long considered to be the birthplace of rock 'n' roll, Sun Studio opened in 1950 and quickly set about recording influential acts such as Howlin' Wolf, BB King, Johnny Cash and, of course, Elvis Presley. Now a historic landmark, the studio also conducts tours, taking visitors through its extraordinary history. The knowledgeable and enthusiastic staff also allow ample time in which to stand in the middle of the original studio used for recording the music that spawned that most incendiary of genres – rock 'n' roll.

BEALE STREET
Memphis, TN 38103; www.bealestreet.com
Located in downtown Memphis, this street is a must for any music lover. While venues and museums line its road, Beale Street is also home to some remarkable attractions. BB King's Blues Club and the Memphis Rock N Soul Museum are among some of the must-sees. Jeff Buckley fans may also like to know that the young guitarist's drowned body was found floating near the foot of this street, days after he went missing in Wolf River Harbor.

BE SEEN

WILD BILL'S

1580 Vollintine Avenue, Memphis, TN 38107

A complete contrast from the lights of Beale Street, Wild Bill's serves up beer in quarts. No extravagant decor here, only hard-backed chairs, long tables and sweaty locals shakin' their tails on the tiny dancefloor. Experience the real Memphis music scene, make new friends and dance yourself senseless. Not for the shy or retiring.

YOUNG AVENUE DELI

2119 Young Avenue, Memphis, TN 38104;
www.youngavenuedeli.com

The best place to hear live music in Memphis, the Deli plays host to both local and touring southern rock and soul bands. With award-winning food, billiards and an impressive selection of beers, the venue is popular with locals and tourists alike. Beer-battered artichoke hearts anyone?

SEELBACH HILTON

~~·◊ᘔ·ᘔᘔᘔ·~~

'I'm sorry, but would you please just SHUT UP?!' The person throwing this Elton-John-sized hissy fit is not some cut-and-dried disconsolate rock star but the usually mellow Norah Jones – a singer famous for her gentle jazz ballads. The cause of Norah's vitriolic outburst was the industry crowd who had gathered noisily at the Seelbach Hilton Hotel for a music convention – a setting that evidently didn't cohere with Jones's plaintive croon as she tried to perform her dulcet songs in the hotel bar.

Billy Joel, on the other hand, must have had more of an attentive crowd as he, reportedly, swiped at the ivories in an impromptu set that lasted nearly five hours when he stayed at the hotel, while on tour with Elton John – who, incidentally, didn't grace the piano with his renowned showmanship. Sir Elton – a dandy with a predilection for all things ornate – was most probably lost in reverence of the Seelbach's own flamboyance: the pop king and the Seelbach are equally unambiguous with their intention to flaunt their formidable ostentation. In short, this hotel is for the well-heeled rock star who's never without a personal entourage or a circus of admirers.

Endowed with elegant vaulted ceilings, decorative columns and intricate mouldings, the hotel renders a scene reminiscent of a hotel lounge from the jazz age, where the sight of a flapper girl would not be incongruous with the hotel's eloquent decor. If this image is vivid in your mind, you can see why F. Scott Fitzgerald – the author credited with coining the 'jazz age' phrase – used the Seelbach as the backdrop for the wedding of the bewitching Buchanan couple in his most famous work *The Great Gatsby*. Fitzgerald himself could often be found at the hotel, puffing on a fat cheroot and sipping Kentucky bourbon; until, that is, he was banned for having supped one too many.

In asserting itself as an awe-inspiring hotel, the Seelbach has imported a hefty amount of marble from across the globe, acquired a sizeable chunk of bronze from France and brought in hardwoods from the West Indies, since its construction in 1903 All this coalesces to create an idealised environment in which guests can relax. It is no wonder, then, that rock artists such as Grateful Dead and Robert Plant chose to forgo their customary debauchery when they stayed here. In fact, despite the wealth of rock bands who have traipsed through the Seelbach's lavish lobby (the hotel claims to have welcomed 14 Grammy-award-winning groups) the most notorious incident came from quite an unlikely source: a teeny-bopper boy-band. In 1991 Donnie Wahlberg, of New Kids on the Block fame, embarked upon an evening of recklessness that would have, no doubt, received nods of approval from rock 'n' roll's most famous hotel-trashing cohorts.

It has been rumoured that Wahlberg had been arguing with a fan and so, having been baited into a rage, went about trying to set the hotel on fire with a Molotov cocktail. As you do. He was charged with first-degree arson and, to evade being locked up, posted $5,000 bail so he could perform at a show later that night. Wahlberg later took part in fire safety public service ads in order to obtain a dismissal of the charge.

Pertinently, as much as a cocktail nearly reduced the Seelbach to ashes, it is a connection with alcohol – the harbinger of rock 'n' roll excess – that forms part of the hotel's illustrious history. Credited with creating the Seelbach Cocktail (a heady mix of bourbon and champagne), the hotel is also known for providing sanctuary to Al Capone – the infamous bootlegger of liquor – so he could drink, play blackjack and make a quick exit through a secret passageway if necessary.

With its ornate motifs and lion-head columns dominating the public areas, the Seelbach may at first glance appear disdainful of all that is modern. However, the rooms are more than sympathetic to the needs of contemporary visitors. Following a $12 million renovation in 2009, guest rooms have been upgraded with new lighting, wall treatments, large HD TVs, data ports and modems. Yet it is where the Seelbach harks to a bygone era that the hotel really excels. With an aura that cedes to its traditional-billiard-hall feel of the early 1900s, The Oakroom is Kentucky's only AAA Five-Diamond restaurant, where you can sample the best Kentucky cuisine and the largest selection of wine in the area.

The Old Seelbach bar, too, evokes the mood of a gentlemen's lounge at the turn of the 19th century. And with several types of bourbon available here, you may well find yourself mimicking Fitzgerald's raucous carousing style, given half the chance.

Seelbach Hilton Hotel, 500 South 4th Street, Louisville, KY 40202, USA

(+1) 502 585 3200
www.seelbachhilton.com

SEE

CHURCHILL DOWNS
700 Central Avenue, Louisville, KY 40208;
www.churchilldowns.com
Get yourself down to this racetrack for a flutter on the horses while sipping champagne from the sides. With weekly prizes for the best-dressed punter and live entertainment, this is the place to see and be seen.

EAR X-TACY
2226 Bardstown Road, Louisville, KY 40205; www.earx-tacy.com
Celebrating 25 years of business in 2010, this well-loved independent record store is much more besides. As well as selling vinyl and CDs, (including lots of hard-to-find releases) it has started up a digital service for mp3s and hosts live bands' sets. There's no entry fee, all gigs are free and feature the best of the local music scene. Finally, don't worry about going up against music snobs here – the staff are great.

BE SEEN

FOURTH STREET LIVE
400 South 4th Street, Louisville, KY 40202; www.4thstlive.com
There's something for everyone at this entertainment, dining and retail complex: Angel's Rock Bar, Rascal's Comedy Bar, a Bourbon House & Lounge, a Hard Rock Café, a live music venue called Howl at the Moon, a saloon and a wealth of restaurants.

THE KENTUCKY CENTER FOR PERFORMING ARTS
501 West Main Street, Louisville, KY 40202;
www.kentuckycenter.org
This all-round performing arts centre showcases a whole host of performers. It has seen everyone from Jim Carrey to the Bolshoi Ballet to latter-day folk hero Josh Ritter. Structurally stunning, acoustically perfect and with an eclectic booking policy, this entertainment complex pulls in the crowds to both the multipurpose 2,406-seat hall and the more intimate theatre.

EUROPE

IBIZA ROCKS

Tell your friends that you're heading off to Ibiza to stay in a rock 'n' roll hotel and you'll probably be met with bemused looks. Tell them you're making a beeline for San Antonio (where the DJ booth once reigned supreme) to catch live sets by a crop of hotly tipped bands currently creating the sort of buzz that leaves music hacks frothing at the mouth, and you'll no doubt prompt hearty laughs from the friends whose bemused and vacant looks quickly turned to mocking smirks.

The White Isle may have once been a dance haven for ravers looking to be rail-roaded into nirvana by way of bangin' beats and bleeps, but Ibiza Rocks Hotel now meets the shift in partygoers' tastes by carrying a stage that holds those most antiquated of band set-ups. Of course, the ravers haven't necessarily conceded defeat (those from the nightclubs' 1980s and 1990s heyday have simply retired and reset their body-clocks to diurnal in order to tend to mortgages, nappies and the school-run) as the island still caters to those looking to blow whistles to the sound of abrasive dance music. Plus, you could argue that this Balearic island has always attracted rock stars to its untroubled shores: Bono and Mick Jagger have often made fleeting party visits; Mike Oldfield (multi-instrumentalist whose music straddles both rock and dance genres) moved to Ibiza in the late 1990s but later sold his mansion to Noel Gallagher, who then subsequently moved out when James Blunt moved in next door and... well, this musical imbroglio could easily become more convoluted than the interband relationships of Fleetwood Mac.

So, enough with the contextualising; how rock 'n' roll is the hotel? Okay, 'young and hip' is probably a fair summation, as this hotel is designed to entertain those who read the *NME*, and not those who subscribe to *Classic Rock* magazine. The dance beats may have fused with guitars and live drums but the 18–30 demographic remains very much the focus. Here the stage is set for indie-rock's new shining lights: Arctic Monkeys, Kasabian, The Enemy, Vampire Weekend, Friendly Fires, The Klaxons and The Virgins are just some of the bands to have roused the hotel's guests, proving this is not merely a novelty boutique hotel but one that is luring acts who are far from being the after-drip of rock 'n' roll. Sure, the clientele may not be keeping the old clichés alive by embarking on hotel rampaging, but this self-proclaimed '24-hour rock 'n' roll hotel' has a slogan that unabashedly declares 'You'll still be rocking when the sun comes up'. Clearly you'll have enough time in which to pickle your innards (the bars never shut) and bed your own groupie (by the way, free condoms are available from reception).

Passing the pool with its huge, submerged plectrum-shaped hotel logo and into the lobby area, you may feel that the hotel becomes more Student Union than Riot House: posters plaster the walls while a bathtub is used as a seating area. You'll find the plectrum logo emblazoned everywhere, most notably on the fluorescent attire sported by the gregarious staff, who flounce about while a DJ spins some tunes, gamely trying to make sure the hotel never has a listless moment, even at 10 in the morning.

The hotel's target audience is teenagers and students, a fact reflected in the room prices (studios for sharing with gig tickets thrown in too), and which subsequently attracts gaggles of school-leavers and graduates. But even if you feel you're past a veritable 'yoof' vibe, there's still not much to get all curmudgeonly over. The rooms are sleek, tastefully appointed and overlook the pool and stage area so, if you're in a studio, you can watch gigs from your balcony. If you're in one of the

uperior Rooms you'll be equipped with an X-Box, plasma TV,
our own terrace from which you'll have a view of the stage and,
st to help with your five-a-day, a bowl of fresh fruit is thrown
too.

Ultimately, though, it's the hotel's dedication to supporting
day's breaking bands that gives the place its *je ne sais quoi*. In
ampioning the new guard, it offers any enterprising guest a
ance to get close to the bands, as the hotel also holds
ter-show parties, boasts its own rehearsal studios and plays
ost to the bands, who, of course, stay in the Penthouse Suite.

Evidently, this is no misguided attempt at bringing live
usic to the clement climes of San Antonio. There is a
a-change happening in Ibiza, and Ibiza Rocks Hotel has been
e first to ride the crest.

iza Rocks Hotel, Carre Estrella 13, 07820 San Antonio,
iza, Spain

44) 020 8133 3930
fo@ibizarockshotel.com
ww.ibizarocks.com/hotel

SEE

ES CANA HIPPY MARKET
Punta Arabi, Es Cana
In the late 60s, while the flower children across the Atlantic were
congregating around Frank Zappa's log cabin in Laurel Canyon,
European hippies were travelling the dusty roads of Ibiza and
settling in Es Cana. Located in the north west of the island, this
legendary hippy market is held on Wednesdays and sells
one-of-a-kind jewellery, pottery, clothing and bags. A boat service
runs to Es Cana from San Antonio.

PAINTBALL LOUNGE PARTY
www.paintballloungeparty.com
If a hippy market doesn't appeal, get your adrenaline fix in this virtual war zone. Blast that hangover by finding the ability to act decisively and think tactically. The ultimate stress-relieving activity!

BE SEEN

THE PINGUIN BAR
Calle Soledad 36, 07820 San Antonio; www.pinguinbar-ibiza.com
If the scene gets a bit too 'indie' at Ibiza Rocks then head to this rock bar. The Dutch and Norwegian owners promise a laidback and friendly atmosphere. Clear out your ears with a blast of some good ol' rock 'n' roll... or some blues... or some metal.

CAFÉ DEL MAR
Calo des Móro, 07820 San Antonio
Huge crowds have been known to line the beach in front of this bar, designed by famous Catalan architect Güell, for the sunset. Enjoy the stunning sunsets over the sea while ambient music wafts out from the café. The café is now better known for its chill-out music compilation albums, of which many volumes have been released.

ME BARCELONA

Ah, Pete Wentz: bass-playing punk elfin who, through his proclivity for entrepreneurship and his former marriage to Ashlee Simpson, quickly became omnipresent celebrity and now garners as much derision as he does admiration. Like a younger, less vaunting, Gene Simmons, but with an emo haircut (traits that led MTV to dub him 'emogul'), Wentz has become quite the polymath: his time now taken up with interests in film and clothing, running his record company (Decaydance) and TV cameo appearances. Plus, there's also the small matter of writing hits for his million-record-selling band Fall Out Boy.

You'd think that having to oversee such ventures would be enough to keep the newly anointed rock entrepreneur busy, but Wentz hasn't put away his branding iron just yet. Launching the first European branch of his Angels & Kings bar on the sixth floor of the ME Barcelona Hotel, Wentz had Fall Out Boy play the opening shindig in October 2008.

Whether you're a fan of Wentz and his music is inconsequential when it comes to enjoying this glamorous drinking den. Far from being the type of hangout in which to hear the latest 'scene' band, the sleek finish of this dark venue attracts the city's elite night owls and, aside from a prison shot of Wentz, there is little that alludes to the bar's famous owner; or his band, for that matter. Paradoxically, you might regard this dimly lit Victorian-inspired locale, with its all-black interior, as the type of drinking haunt that perfectly encapsulates the furnished gloom closely associated with emo music. Yet, to ensure guests don't feel as though they've been entombed in some subterranean cave, the bar is lifted by a terrace with a swimming pool and superb views over the city.

Which brings us neatly to the Dos Cielos restaurant on the 24th floor, which is as much about the panorama as it is the food. Lucky gourmands are treated to 360° views; it's easy to while away an evening marvelling at the city twinkling below, flanked by mountains on one side and the Mediterranean on the other. Pacified diners will soon feel their pulses quicken if they've prescribed to the quintessential rock-star maxim of 'biggest is best' and booked the Sky Suite, which takes up the entire 29th floor. Available to discerning rockers looking for a hedonistic package to match their rock-star posturing, it comes with a butler, and a wealth of amenities – huge interactive plasma TV, Wii and PlayStation, a personalised service from the Everything is Possible service team and access to the exclusive club lounge on the 25th floor.

Just beneath the sumptuous Sky Suite sits what is known as The Level. Taking up floors 20–28, the suites here are nothing to be sniffed at. Offering the same amenities as the Sky Suite, the Supreme Rooms are split into City View and Sea View categories, but both types manage a characterful blend of metallic sheen and soft whites with splashes of colour. Elsewhere on The Level, Loft Suites boast comfortable lounge areas, while the luxuriously spacious Urban Suites feature spectacular views of the Mediterranean.

Even if you're not a rock star, this hotel certainly knows how to make you feel like one. And, of all the packages currently available, Your Entourage Pass seems to be best suited to rock-star wannabes. Providing services such as a champagne pick-up from the airport, a Bloody Mary bar in your room and VIP club access, it also, thankfully, has a late check-out option. Keeping things playful, the One-On-One for Two package delivers the romance with a champagne pick-up from the airport, a gift certificate for a romantic dinner and a do-not-disturb passion pack.

ME Barcelona also delivers more glitz by way of its Sky Lounge Bar, which mirrors the ethereal quality of the Mondrian's Sky Bar in Los Angeles, being swathed in white and exuding a similar swanky charm. It hasn't attracted the same sort of exclusive clientele just yet, but word is beginning to spread that ME Barcelona is quickly becoming the hotspot for those who want to drink, dance and stay somewhere that has glamour and the cinematic allure of LA's sun-kissed invincibility and magnetism. Yet, don't expect to bump into a plethora of Hollywood A-listers; the hotel, despite its sheen, isn't so *mainstream* as that. Instead, being an achingly hip hotel means it's the musicians at rock 'n' roll's acute cutting edge that are lured to the swanky environs. For example, melancholia's poet Nick Cave and fellow Bad Seeds and Soundtrack sidekick Warren Ellis have been spotted eating lunch there, while noise-rocker Bradford Cox (vocalist for Deerhunter) and instrumental experimentalists Explosions in the Sky have also been seen loitering in fashionably cool repose. In other words, this is the place where it's okay to wear your shades indoors.

ME Barcelona Hotel, Carrer Pere IV 272, 08005 Barcelona, Spain

(+34) 902 14 44 40
mebarcelona@solmelia.com
www.me-barcelona.com

SEE

LE MERIDIEN BARCELONA
La Rambla 111, 08002 Barcelona; www.lemeridienbarcelona.es
Located on the famous Las Ramblas, this swanky hotel has
accommodated all the top stars: Madonna, Bruce Springsteen and
Michael Jackson. Chart-toppers continue to check-in here too,
making the elegant Cent Onze Bar a great place to while away the
hours over the course of a few cocktails and some celeb-watching.

BARRIO GÓTICO (GOTHIC QUARTER)
The Gothic Quarter, the centre of the old town, is a fascinating
place in which to lose yourself. A labyrinth of medieval buildings
built on Roman foundations, the area is home to hundreds of
unusual shops and small bars. Its narrow streets are packed 24 hours
a day.

BE SEEN

BAR MARSELLA
Carrer de Sant Pau 65, El Raval, 08001 Barcelona
Open from 10p.m. until 3a.m., Friday and Saturday (and
10–2.30a.m. Monday to Thursday), this bohemian hangout was
once frequented by the likes of Hemingway and Picasso. Located in
the old part of town, the bar stands in testament to the area's
former heyday as the place in which nonconformists could discuss
their iconoclastic ideas and drink absinthe. You can still come here
and dance with the green fairy, by the way.

BIKINI
*Deu I Mata 105 and Avenida Diagonal 547, 08029 Barcelona;
www.bikinibcn.com*
Bikini is a popular Barcelona venue for rock and indie music. With
separate rooms for Latin rhythms and rock, the club also has a
cocktail bar tucked away. No need to leave when the band finishes
playing, as you can dance the night away once the DJ starts up.

HOTEL MARTINEZ

In his book *Kill Your Friends* John Niven depicts a cut-throat music industry run by myriad coke-snorting, champagne-guzzling, self-serving opportunists who leach and snipe at every turn in order to have a shot at becoming high-rollers – a business practice symptomatic of the industry's tangible success in the mid 1990s. In truth, it was a beautiful era for the record industry: a time before the Internet made music ubiquitous and when record companies could charge full whack for a CD and benefit from the subsequent huge profit margins.

Although the book is fiction, Niven reportedly drew heavily on his experience of working in A&R for a (now defunct) major label. In pursuit of the 'next big thing' Niven readily admits that, together with other young sharks, he travelled to conventions feigning the role of a consummate businessman to 'play the game' with barely functioning drug fiends who, collectively, believed they could dictate what the country would be listening to in a year's time.

If the Internet has stuck a shiv in the face of the music business, then it hasn't abated the clinking of champagne flutes or the phalanx at the renowned music convention MIDEM (or le Marché International du Disque et de l'Edition Musicale). Every year a glut of musicians, journalists and an assortment of industry types are dispatched to the music trade fair at Cannes' Palais des Festivals, which sits just in front of Hotel Martinez. Suffice to say, given the hotel's positioning, it has received its fair share of unalloyed partying since MIDEM's inception in 1967. After the conferences, showcases and unveilings are done, a throng of label reps, tailed by enterprising musicians, fill the hotel's bar and lobby for more networking, back-slapping and, of course, drinking.

But it's not just company head-honchos that descend upon the Riviera every January. Breaking up some of the interminable conferences are live showcases. Britain's very own lady of decadence, Amy Winehouse, put in a memorable performance at the hotel itself while, over the years, everything from the cacophony of Captain Beefheart to the two-tone of The Specials to the heavy-metal cello-play of Finnish rockers Apocalyptica, has graced the stages.

That said, even if you're not heading to the Martinez to hawk round a record bag of demos at MIDEM, you'll still find yourself yielding to a palpable sense of chic rock 'n' roll that exists even without the chutzpah of a music fair. Situated on the eminent Boulevard de la Croisette, the Martinez, with its art-deco decor, seems to presage an intoxicating night of cocktail glam. Consider the two-Michelin-starred restaurant La Palme d'Or, the elegant Le Relais or the piano bar where even the serving staff are the crème de la crème of waiters, and it doesn't take too much of an imaginative leap to comprehend how easy is for a horde of musicians and A&R scouts to enter the hotel with every intention of executing a deal only to flounder under the influence and return home with just a hangover.

The Suite des Oliviers will rouse anyone's inner rock star. With an enormous private terrace with views across the iridescent Cannes, it amply displays rock-star living. Lounging in its jacuzzi with room for seven, you'll feel like a young David Geffen schmoozing with the next big rock act. The Penthouse Prestige Apartments, too, prove to be the perfect habitat for rock stars and music moguls. Comprising two terrace-apartments that house, among other things, two bedrooms, two bathrooms, a spa bath and a sauna, this set-up also comes with prestigious view overlooking the shimmering Bay of Cannes and out towards the Lérins Islands. And as you would expect, all the required state-of-the-art technology is here and a butler service is available throughout your stay, while the warm decor is conducive to rest and recharging, following your dissemination among the mass of industry bods. But if the synapses feel perpetually charged, take yourself off to the Spa Martinez, where a peaceful milieu promises to soothe throbbing heads.

Much like applying for a slot at a festival, you submit your songs to MIDEM and await a response (check MIDEM's website for further info). Then, the next thing you know you too could be abetting the myths of the Martinez yourself.

Hotel Martinez, 73 Boulevard de la Croisette, 06400 Cannes, France

+33) 4 92 98 73 00
www.hotel-martinez.com

SEE

PALAIS DES FESTIVALS
Boulevard de la Croisette, 06414 Cannes;
www.palaisdesfestivals.com
For the obvious reasons, this is *the* place to network and schmooze when MIDEM is in town. With increased numbers each year, this is where music companies from all over the world head to secure exclusive deals. If you're in a band, you should be applying for tickets.

ST MARGUERITE ISLAND
If you fancy something on the dark side, take a trip to the Lérins Islands (a 15-minute boat ride) which include St Marguerite Island. Visit the cell in the Fort of St Marguerite (renamed Museum of the Sea) where the Man in the Iron Mask was held for 11 years during the late 17th century. His identity is still a mystery...

BE SEEN

BOULEVARD DE LA CROISETTE

The long arc of the main seafront of Cannes, extending eastwards from the Palais des Festivals, is where you'll be able to view the stars who have just popped into town. Strut your rock-star look as you weave in and out of high-class shops before hitting the beach.

BAR LE BARRACUDA

22 rue Latour-Maubourg, 06400 Cannes

Just behind the famous La Croisette, this popular hangout for musos and moguls has a selective door policy, so classy-chic is the recommended dress code. Open until dawn, this is the hippest bar in town and will most likely see you sipping a cocktail alongside a celebrity.

THE INTERCONTINENTAL
CARLTON CANNES

n army of dancers line the wide walkway that leads up to a set
Doric columns framing the entrance of a palatial building.
he dancers' toned bodies – painted with stripes of electric blue,
nny yellow and blood red – move in unison as muscles ripple
d slender limbs nimbly bend and bow with all the vim and
gour of a Broadway musical. They thrust their arms skyward as
ton John, decked out in a red suit and boater, swaggers
tween them, with all the confidence of a man who knows he
making a music video for what will be his next hit single.

Indeed, said music video, shot in the sunny climes of the
ench Riviera, did herald a hit on both sides of the Atlantic for
r Elton. The song was 'I'm Still Standing' and the palatial
ilding featured in the video was what's known today as The
terContinental Carlton Cannes.

If you've seen the video, you'll know that once Elton has
ached the grand entrance of the hotel, the video cuts to a
retch of beach where he croons his 'yeah-yeah-yeahs' amid a
rightly throng of dancers that look as if they were culled from
e cast of 1980 hit musical film *Fame*. The camera then turns
s lens away from the sapphire sea, and the performers
vorting in the sand, to show the jaw-dropping ivory grandeur
The Carlton peering over the treelined boulevard that borders
e beach.

If you want to fully comprehend the awe-inspiring opulence
The Carlton before setting foot on Boulevard de la Croisette,
e're going to have to flash forward 10 years to New
rder's 1993 song 'World (The Price of Love)'. This promo

video starts at the pier, the sheer scale of the hotel's white exterior filling the frame with the two large crowning domes – reputedly inspired by the breasts of famous courtesan La Belle Otero – just about visible in the shot. The steadicam then leads us towards the towering facade as it weaves through the affluent tourists, past bassist Peter Hook (sat slouched at a table) and into the hotel itself, where we are greeted with yet more Doric columns. Holding onto the trail, the camera pans slowly and stealthily, as if some voyeuristic concierge treating us to a sneak preview of the vintage luxury that lies within these hallowed walls.

The song's steady electronic pulse keeps us engaged as we are lead up a grand wide staircase and down hallways of old-world charm in what is evidently the very definition of a classic hotel. As we are tentatively guided down a corridor of a stately room, we glimpse the vista of the sea through parted curtains.

Of course, as much as New Order's video offers a visual precis, you can't beat the reality of checking-in to experience a service that can accommodate the most testing of requests. Past challenges for the most savvy of staff have included a princess with 120 suitcases and a guest who ordered 100 kilometres of barbed wire from the concierge. Cannes Film Festival, every May, brings with it a full quota of celebs; but even their demands don't result in arched eyebrows from the staff here. With splendour emanating from every corner, The Carlton is more inclined to entertain the likes of Madonna and her requests for 'special' water (made when she was in Cannes promoting *I Am Because We Are*, her documentary about orphans in Malawi) or provide the setting for a movie in which the romantic trysts are played out against the hotel's marble background (as was the case for Cary Grant and Grace Kelly in Hitchcock's film *To Catch a Thief*).

The Carlton's beauty has echoed down the years and continues to attract the glitterati to its 40 suites, each named after top celebrities. The recently renovated Standard Rooms also lure the top players by way of oozing 1950s Hollywood glamour.

Evidently, then, this is a hotel for the stars in the upper-echelons of celebrity and not the nefarious types occupying the lower rungs. That is to say it is for the elegantly wasteful, not the elegantly wasted.

The InterContinental Carlton Cannes, 58 Boulevard de la Croisette, 06406 Cannes, France

(+33) 4 93 06 40 06
carlton@ihg.com
www.intercontinental.com

SEE

CANNES FILM FESTIVAL
www.festival-cannes.fr
One of the world's most prominent film festivals, this annual celebration of lights, camera, action! takes place at the Palais des Festivals, meaning that, for two weeks in May, Cannes is overrun with celebrities and their parties. This huge film-fest celebrates the heritage of film, new films, short films, the talents of newcomers and, well, just about every aspect of film. In addition to the programming by the Cannes Film Festival, outside organisations also arrange the Directors' Fortnight and International Critics' Week.

VIEUX-PORT
Cannes Harbour
It's a classic case of seeing how the other half live. Wander past the world-class yachts and lose yourself in a rich-list reverie. If you want to take a step towards such dreams, then you could always hire a plush yacht (www.classyacht.com) or just make do with admiring them, if you come in September, at the Cannes International Boat and Yacht Show.

BE SEEN

LES PRINCES CASINO BARRIÈRE DE CANNES
50 Boulevard de la Croisette, 06400 Cannes;
www.lucienbarriere.com
Experience a world of dreams and high emotions at one of the
several casinos in Cannes. Les Princes is the most extravagant,
eschewing slot machines for traditional roulette, poker and blackjack
tables. Or just stroll around dressed up to the nines with an air of
nonchalance.

LE BÂOLI
Port Pierre Canto, Boulevard de la Croisette, 06400 Cannes;
www.lebaoli.com
This luxury restaurant promises to transport you to another world
with its exotic decor and subtle blend of traditional and Asian
flavours. The initially chilled-out atmosphere develops into full-on
party as the night goes on.

L'HÔTEL

You may well know that Jim Morrison and Oscar Wilde share the same resting place – the Père-Lachaise Cemetery in Paris – but did you know that they also once shared the same bed? Obviously they weren't between the sheets at the same time – more than 70 years passed between Oscar planting his coiffured head on the pillow and Jim resting his shaggy mane on the same headboard – but, nevertheless, both renegade poets slept in Room 16 at L'Hôtel.

In May 1971 (just months before Jim's death) Morrison and his long-time girlfriend, Pamela Courson, checked into L'Hôtel. The hotel, and Room 16 in particular, would have held considerable appeal for the then hirsute and bloated Jim Morrison, who was quite au fait with his decadent aesthetes. After all, Morrison, too, fancied himself as something of a rebellious belletrist, having turned his back on the Lizard King gig in order to pursue literary ambitions. He would have, no doubt, felt in good company under the spectral gaze of Mr Wilde.

The chic and luxurious furnishings, fit for distinguished libertines, will also have held gravitas for Morrison. Indeed, there is a whiff of Wilde's dandyish flair in L'Hôtel: plump velvet cushions, heavy drapes over sumptuous beds, and iridescent displays of colour pervade. Amazingly, the decor doesn't come across as a gaudy blunder but, instead, manages a certain dignified charm as it segues from rococo to classic English styles, with no room exactly like another. It's almost as if L'Hôtel were designed by a clique of English aristocrats with a predilection for foreign design. The Mistinguett Room, named after the French singer and actress, exudes art-deco glamour and features her original furniture. The room also has flapper girls decorating the walls, a mirrored bed, and tall French windows. Elsewhere, rooms feature oriental motifs and flourishes of art nouveau, as evinced in the now-called Oscar Wilde Room. In paying tribute to Wilde, the room features portraits of the famous playwright, a number of handwritten letters and a peacock mural, as Wilde was prone to decorating his rooms with peacock feathers during his stay.

When Oscar Wilde arrived at L'Hôtel – then known as Hôtel d'Alsace – in August 1899, the hotel was considered to be something of a disreputable place to stay. Finding it less than a bastion of sophistication, Wilde famously opined 'either the wallpaper goes, or I do!' Not that Wilde would have been able to afford anywhere else: he was nearly penniless and in self-imposed exile following a treacherous stint in prison. Wilde reached his nadir during his stay at the hotel as both his health and his financial situation worsened. Trading on these facts, the hotel has placed a letter, requesting that Mr Wilde see to it that his hotel bill is paid, above the writing desk in Room 16, but he died owing over 26,000 francs.

By the 1960s, however, this now-boutique hotel had become something of a draw for the upper-crust louche, and since then Al Pacino, Lenny Kravitz, Frank Sinatra and Quentin Tarantino have all passed through the lavish lobby where Oscar Wilde uttered his last quip. The hotel's allure is evident from the moment you pass the Oscar Wilde plaque at the entrance and step into the lobby, where a magnificent spiral staircase lithely winds its way up to the 20 guest rooms over six floors. But, the decadence really hits home when you venture down into the cellar, where a candle-lit roman bath, perfect for a romantic liaison, awaits.

The bar provides a further hedonistic touch with its dusky atmosphere. This dimly lit snug casts shadows across a ritzy

Louis XIV-style bar, adorned with pictures of Johnny Depp and Mick Jagger – just a few of the bar's illustrious guests. The hotel's restaurant is equally sumptuous with marble columns, velvet seating, leopard-print rugs and soft lighting.

A secret hideaway oozing Parisian glamour, L'Hôtel offers one of the most opulent stays in Paris. From its location, within the artistic haven that is the Left Bank, you can easily trace the steps of famous musicians, writers and philosophers as they sipped absinthe and put the world to rights.

L'Hôtel, 13 rue des Beaux-Arts, 75006 Paris, France
(+33) 1 44 41 99 00
stay@l-hotel.com
www.l-hotel.com

SEE

LE CIMETIÈRE DU PÈRE-LACHAISE (PÈRE-LACHAISE CEMETERY)
16 rue du Repos, 75020 Paris; www.pere-lachaise.com
The final resting place for Jim Morrison (as well as many other poets, writers and musicians), this is one of the most famous cemeteries in the world. Many fans still make the pilgrimage to Jim's grave and pay their respects by way of leaving letters, cigarettes and candles.

LEFT BANK CAFÉS
Traditional cafés on the Left Bank are where artists and writers still work, discuss ideas and consume. See if you can soak up the Parisian boho vibe while sipping a *café crème* or *verre de vin blanc* at any time of the day or night.

BE SEEN

CAVEAU DE LA HUCHETTE
5 rue de la Huchette, 75005 Paris; www.caveaudelahuchette.fr
This jazz club is located just around the corner from L'Hôtel in the Latin Quarter. A converted medieval cellar, the venue not only has

an intimate, humid atmosphere and fantastic sound system, but also a colourful history. Dating back to the 16th century, the cellar is said to have been used by a secret society of mystics.

LA SOCIÉTÉ
4 Place Saint Germain, 75006 Paris; www.restaurantlasociete.com
This very hip and exclusive restaurant is located in a 19th-century farm building. Designer Christian Liaigre has bedecked the interior with sumptuous materials such as marble, leather and mahogany. Lobster on the menu – what else?

GEORGE V

Music journalists are reviled and revered in equal measure; unsuspecting scribes can find themselves in the most inclement situations, sometimes after only the briefest of dalliances with rock 'n' roll's rogues. One wrong word upsetting a fragile ego can result in receiving a turd in the post. Or, as was the case with rock journo Mick Wall, in being told to 'get in the ring motherfucker', by the flame-haired Axl Rose. No, life's not easy for a journo.

Sticking with the tribulations of the aforementioned Mr Wall, it was he who was once sent to interview the mighty Black Sabbath, in Paris. Tucked away at the George V (the V is pronounced 'sank') – a hotel veneered in the type of opulence usually reserved for the Palace of Versailles – the eager hack had become acquainted with each of the heavy metal titans over the course of a weekend. All except one, that is. The band's drummer, Bill Ward, had proved elusive. The common cold was the reason given for Bill's ominous absence, but the reality was that he was inebriated after fondling the bottle a bit too keenly. As Mick prepared for his departure, Sabbath interview notes packed, *sans* Bill Ward quotes, the credulous reporter was summoned. At 2a.m., Mick entered Bill's suite to find a sweaty, semi-naked drummer lost in a stupor. With his dressing gown falling open as he drunkenly staggered about the room, Bill treated Mick to a glimpse of his genitals and a playback of the song 'Neon Knights', before barking at the poor writer a barrage of expletives that would make even Ozzy sound like a God-fearing saint in comparison.

But even when rock stars aren't berating their scribbling guests, journalists can still end up having a bad time. Take

Lenny Kaye for example. He entered the George V's gilded lobby, crossing its polished marble floors, to make his way to the Louis XIV-styled suite that Alice Cooper was occupying and helped himself to the oysters and lobsters provided. It was an evening that ended in abdominal tragedy, as the ink-slinger had to make a quick retreat to his own less-than-salubrious hotel room and fasten himself to the rim of his porcelain throne.

Nevertheless, the life of a rock star, too, has its dangers. In fact, the three pillars of rock-star living – sex, drugs and rock 'n' roll – can prove so virulent and contagious that the hangers-on, too, can end up in the tailspin. A case in point is Pamela Courson – Jim Morrison's long-time auburn muse. She checked into one of the George V's alluring suites, in Europe's most romantic city, on Valentine's Day, only to embark on a drug-fuelled sex session with a French aristocrat. The aristocrat in question was Jean de Breteuil, a self-proclaimed 'dealer to the stars' and a man whom Morrison disliked due to his penchant for drugs (although an incorrigible alcoholic, Morrison's own drug intake at this juncture had abated considerably) and his affection for Pamela. However, it is understood that both Jim and Pamela were snorting heroin bought from Breteuil on the night Jim died in July 1971. After Morrison's death, the French playboy swiftly fled to Morocco, with new girlfriend Marianne Faithful in tow.

Of course, not all rock 'n' roll moil leaves you falling apart at the seams. The travails could simply result in missing a connecting flight one morning following an evening spent drinking with songsmith Jacques Brel (an incident experienced by David Bowie when he checked into the George V in 1973). After all, it's not difficult to fall prey to the liquor when staying at this hotel. The high-end drinking establishment here, known simply as Le Bar, is filled with ornate furniture that exudes an

a of a bygone era but, nevertheless, delivers cocktails with a
odern twist, served by attentive staff.

When The Beatles stayed here in 1964 they had two
allenges: to look achingly hip (not hard) and to follow up
eir recent hit with an equally catchy melody to capture the
tion's hearts. Having had a huge smash in America in 1963
th 'I Want to Hold Your Hand', the Fab Four were expected
continually dole out the hits, even when they were on tour.
, while holed up in the George V, an upright piano was
eeled into McCartney's suite, where the young Beatle
oceeded to write their next American winner 'Can't Buy Me
ve'.

But can the above careers really be deemed that arduous?
ell, when compared with that of a hotelier, the job of a rock
rno or rock star is a breeze. Upholding the exceptionally high
ndards of a plush hotel that has won a number of awards
m *Condé Nast Traveller* and even welcomed the King of rock
yalty, Elvis Presley, on his single European visit (outside of his
litary service, that is) is quite a feat. And that's because, in
ort, George V is the paragon of grace in the City of Love.
us, it can't be good for the nerves having to continually ensure
at Jack Daniels doesn't get spilled on your 17th-century
estries.

**ur Seasons Hotel George V, 31 Avenue George V, 75008
ris, France**
33) 1 49 52 70 00
ww.fourseasons.com/paris

SEE

MOULIN ROUGE
82 Boulevard de Clichy, 75018 Paris; www.moulinrouge.fr
Famous for its can-can courtesans, its fame was brought to a more modern audience in 2001 by the Baz Luhrmann film *Moulin Rouge*. Located near Montmartre, this place is difficult to miss, as its huge red mill is lit up like a Vegas casino. That said, it's not difficult to imagine the bacchanalian vibe of the can-can's heyday given that the cabaret club has retained much of its original 19th century decadent decor. Unsurprisingly, many latter-day divas such as Liza Minelli, La Toya Jackson and the biggest diva of them all, Sir Elton John, have dropped by to entertain.

RALPH LAUREN
173 Boulevard Saint Germain, 75006 Paris; see www.ralphlauren.fr
No rock 'n' roll lifestyle would be complete without some emptying of wallets on a massive scale. Check out the top floor of this branch of the beloved US brand, which has been designed on a Wild West theme. Yeehah cowboy!

BE SEEN

HÔTEL RITZ PARIS
15 Place Vendôme, 75041 Paris; www.ritzparis.com
Another rock 'n' roll haunt that would probably be very grateful if you tried not to emulate any Mötley Crüe antics; this prestigious hotel once had its glass doors kicked in by an intoxicated Vince Neil. Instead, take a seat in Bar Hemingway, peruse the photographs of Ernest and drink one for old Papa H, and just hang around – as you're likely to see a few rock stars sauntering through here too.

CHACHA CLUB
47 rue Berger, 75001 Paris; www.chachaclub.fr
This uber-trendy club, bar and restaurant is *the* place where models and designers congregate during Fashion Week and where rock bands such as Oasis have hosted after-show parties. If the leather surroundings, custom-made wallpaper and candelabras don't impress, there is always the VIP-only bedroom. Nibbles such as tapas and antipasti are available, but people don't come here for the food.

THE CLARENCE

What do you do once you've sold millions of albums, performed packed-out venues the world over and stayed in some of the very best hotels? Well, you buy your own of course.

Bankrolled by a consortium of investors including U2's Bono and the Edge, the restoration of a hotel that has had its prime place on the River Liffey since 1852 began in earnest in the early 1990s, with the two rock stars ensuring the rock 'n' roll touches were all present and correct.

There's much to suggest that their collective vision – albeit from behind wrap-around-shades and beneath beanie hat – has been executed with the same sort of resolute approach afforded their lofty musical endeavours. Not to say that The Clarence is home to the huge TV-stage-sets or the mirrorball lemon or any other prop that has made U2's live shows such brazen and bold affairs. And neither will you find the walls adorned with gold records or with pictures of Bono hanging out with the Pope.

Instead, the elder statesmen of rock have gone for something a tad more restrained and steadfastly created a pristine, striking contemporary citadel that still retains some of its original Georgian beauty. The requisite rock-star pad is the penthouse suite, which features an outdoor jacuzzi on its rooftop terrace, a baby grand piano, complimentary champagne and an entertainment system with access to 4,500 music tracks, which is always worth sifting through should you tire of sipping pink champagne in the Tea Room Restaurant. No doubt you'll come across a U2 track or two as you shuffle through the songs.

The Clarence Hotel, 6–8 Wellington Quay, Dublin 2, Ireland

(+353) 01 407 0800
reservations@theclarence.ie
www.theclarence.ie

SEE

VICAR STREET
58 Thomas Street, Dublin 2; www.vicarstreet.com
Fans of Josh Ritter, The Frames, Mundy or all three will know the name of this popular venue. You may even own one of these artists' live albums recorded at Vicar Street. As reputable as the aforementioned artists are, they're certainly not the biggest names to have graced the stage here. Despite (or maybe because of) the fairly intimate size (1,000 standing, 1,600 seating), Vicar Street has managed to pull in world-class acts such as Bob Dylan, Neil Young, James Brown and Nick Cave. Sited a stone's throw from The Clarence Hotel, this much-admired local venue also promises a great night out with its stand-up comedy nights.

BRUXELLES
7–8 Harry Street, Dublin 2; www.bruxelles.ie
Dublin's most famous rock 'n' roll pub is one you can't miss given the statue of Thin Lizzy frontman Phil Lynott at the entrance, signalling this place out as one in which you can enjoy some classic rock. But this bar has a lot more than an awesome jukebox. It has a remarkable history too. As well as being the favoured watering hole for the aforementioned Lynott, the bar has also witnessed Rolling Stone guitarist Ronnie Wood take to the stage with a young Imelda May on backing vocals. And who was in the crowd watching? Only Axl Rose and Slash of Guns N' Roses, in their glory days. Other acts to have dropped in for a pint: Iron Maiden, Oasis, AC/DC, Anthrax, Paul Weller, Bryan Adams, James Dean Bradfield, Bruce Springsteen, John Denver (just a week before his death)… oh, this could go on forever.

BE SEEN

THE BUTTON FACTORY

Temple Bar Music Centre, Curved Street, Temple Bar, Dublin 2;
www.buttonfactory.ie

Making its debut on Dublin's music scene in late 2007, this venue is a standout thanks to a top lighting rig and state of the art PA. Following a recent refurb, the venue has increased its capacity and augmented the balcony space. Sitting within Dublin's cultural district aka the Temple Bar area, the Button Factory is in a prime location for revellers. The venue stages everything from DJ nights to rock bands to free-form jazz nights. But whatever is on, the high stage means a good line of sight for all.

THE TEMPLE BAR

47–48 Temple Bar, Dublin 2; www.thetemplebarpub.com

Described as the Best Bar in the World, Temple Bar doesn't offer much in the way of solitude. With its warm welcome, good craic, beer garden, live (highly contagious) music every day and a Wall of Fame, what's not to love? Located on the south bank of the River Liffey in an area full of character and cobbled streets, the bar also has a popular steak and seafood restaurant.

PARR STREET

From Coldplay to Carcass, New Order to Napalm Death, and
Gomez to Echo & the Bunnymen, all have committed their art
to tape at Parr Street Studios. There's not enough space to list
all the acts that have left an indelible mark in the annals of rock
after recording at Parr Street, but there is room for mentioning
one more in particular – a group of acid-drenched rockers going
by the name of The Brian Jonestown Massacre.

Having been the subject of the award-winning documentary
Dig! in 2004 – in which we see the BJM's volatile vocalist,
Anton Newcombe, intent on existing in a mêlée with the record
industry, gig audiences and even his own band members – the
group was propelled to cult status. When they arrived at Parr
Street Studios to cut 'My Bloody Underground', the unsavoury
antics had hardly abated: Anton, forever the incorrigible
drug-addled egotist, indulged his appetite for psychedelic drugs
and imposed a 'no talking in the studio' policy. Then, having
obviously tired of Liverpool's perpetual honouring of its famous
four mop-tops, via the many Beatles-themed attractions, the
BJM recorded a song titled 'Bring Me the Head of Paul
McCartney on Heather Mills' Wooden Peg (Dropping Bombs
on The White House)' before transferring studio sessions to
Reykjavik and Berlin.

With Grammies galore, Parr Street Studios has a
convoluted history, which has seen it survive a fire and stave off
closure (former owner Phil Collins wanted to turn the complex
into apartments), while all the time accommodating mellifluous
divas and cacophonous death metallers. Parr Street was a
recording facility long before it added accommodation, which
brings a certain authenticity to Parr Street's boutique hotel

(which can sometimes be lacking in those hotels that add studios in an attempt to ascribe to a rock 'n' roll aesthetic). Parr Street needn't strive to be rock 'n' roll, it *is* rock 'n' roll; its sacrosanct walls still reverberate with the spirited sound of both established and new artists plying their trade, as supporting music is integral to Parr Street's *raison d'être*.

The palpable energy is not reserved for just those on 'muso' business either. Studio 2 (the studio in which Elbow once recorded) has been hewn into a bar, with the recording engineers' control room being the service area. Studio boffins may be impressed to know that they have retained the original control room glass (which looks out into the main room) and the two old drum rooms, with its authenticity now augmented with beanbags and gothic furnishings. And, as you would expect, there is ample space for live music.

Another hot spot for drinks is 3345. This restaurant and lounge area has proved to be a popular haunt for locals and has seen the likes of Feeder and the Doves sampling the wine selection. Rumour also has it that Gwyneth Paltrow was spotted here accompanying her husband Chris Martin on Coldplay-related business. What's more, 3345 has a boardroom for holding meetings or hosting album playback events (previous clients include Richard Ashcroft and, again, Coldplay; they evidently love it here at Parr Street).

The 12 en suite rooms were once reserved solely for artists recording at the studios. Now, having been revamped into distinctive stripped-down-chic accommodation, they are available to all. As well as stylish black-and-white-tiled bathrooms, guests can also expect funky leather sleigh beds, Fatboy beanbags and a fridge with complimentary mini-bar. It's a fresh, contemporary approach that will appeal to those looking for something different from homogenous chain hotels. The oms are still booked by visiting artists, so don't be surprised to imp into a famous musician ambling down the corridor.

Fledgling artists should take note: this revered hub of eativity is proactive in its support of live music. An industry owcase is held every Monday evening at 3345, at which artists e encouraged to ingratiate themselves with industry types. Parr reet has also been known to promote a 'school of rock' night, esigned to help local musicians get to one of the most nportant international festivals of the year: South by Southwest XSW) in Texas.

Clearly, there's a creative force managing Parr Street, one at has a distinct commitment to promoting music. It seems to : an ethos ingrained within their approach. Long may it ntinue.

urr Street Hotel, 33–45 Parr Street, Liverpool L1 4JN, UK

44) 0151 707 1050
fo@parrstreet.co.uk
ww.parrstreet.co.uk

SEE

THE BEATLES STORY
Britannia Vaults, Albert Dock, Liverpool L3 4AD;
www.beatlesstory.com
Housed within the Albert Dock (see page 125), this museum deserves a separate mention. It is the only museum dedicated entirely to The Beatles, their astronomical rise and their impact on popular culture. You'll need to allow a couple of hours while in this neck of the woods to cram everything in.

WORLD MUSEUM
William Brown Street, Liverpool L3 8EN;
www.liverpoolmuseums.org.uk/wml
Pop on your cultural hat for a wander around the World Museum, which includes exhibits on, well, the entire world. The top floor,

covering space and time, features real rockets and a planetarium; so sit back and enjoy a trip that's out of this world.

BE SEEN

THE CAVERN
10 Mathew Street, Liverpool L2 6RE; www.cavernclub.org
The club in which Brian Epstein first saw The Beatles. Ultimately, it was the four mop-tops who made the Cavern famous, but the tiny club also saw the likes of The Rolling Stones, The Who, The Yardbirds and The Kinks take to the stage. Oh, and, erm, Cilla Black, too.

ALMA DE CUBA
St Peter's Church, Seel Street, Liverpool L1 4BH; www.alma-de-cuba.com
Rock-star wannabes hang out in their packs here, especially at weekends when it can get mightily crowded. You can't help but be blown away by the spectacular setting of Alma de Cuba: in a converted church, still featuring the original stained-glass windows but with newly added enormous chandeliers and splendid decor. The cuisine is Latin and Cuban, and so are the rhythms. Come for a weekend brunch to the sounds of a live gospel choir or arrive before 11p.m. at weekends, when they release clouds of rose petals from the balcony restaurant into the bar below.

HARD DAYS NIGHT

With no complex camera tricks and no rock-star preening, the music video for one of the best songs in the world is simplicity itself. John Lennon sits at a white piano singing a plaintive melody, gently urging us to imagine the world as a united harmonious entity, free of the boundaries set by religion and politics. Meanwhile, Yoko Ono, enrobed in white, walks about the room opening tall white shutters, allowing the light to flood in and reveal a room of ethereal beauty.

The video was filmed at Tittenhurst Park – Lennon and Ono's deferential Georgian manor house – and its white piano became synonymous with Lennon's 'Imagine'. And now, those with an abiding fascination with the enduring song of peace, and its accompanying video, can sample their own bit of simple harmony.

Similarly bathed in white, the Lennon Suite at Hard Days Night Hotel draws upon the connotations of peace and purity in the iconic 'Imagine' video. The requisite white piano sits by a large window through which daylight pours into an airy room adorned with deep white armchairs while the white walls are lined with John Lennon portraits. The suite may not boast views of lush green, like those at Tittenhurst (we're obviously not in the same genteel setting), but the astute Beatles fan will notice that the hotel is located in Liverpool's famous 'Beatles Quarter'. This vantage point means that you don't have to take a long and winding road to explore the Fab Four's birthplace. And what could be more pertinent a place to stage your own bed-in as the room price includes a champagne breakfast for two? On that note, Lennon may have sang 'all you need is love' but for this suite you'll need much more since it racks up to about £950 per night.

The other penthouse suite in this four-star boutique hotel is, of course, the McCartney Suite. In paying homage to the former mop-top, the suite features a newspaper collage made up of headline-grabbing articles on Macca and a suit of armour, providing a cheeky nod towards Sir Paul's knighthood. Exclusive artwork and Sir Paul's certificate of Freedom of the City of Liverpool are also some of the features that will appease the diehard McCartney fan looking to get closer to their hero in this vibrant suite.

The Beatles' fame is referenced in other parts of the hotel, too, including the exterior. As you approach the hotel, four statues loom large on its Victorian frontage. On closer inspection, you'll recognise the sculptures to be casts of the Fab Four posing with guitars. Once inside this reformed Grade II-listed building, you'll find yourself flanked by unique Beatles art, the most impressive of which are the black-and-white photographs that line the walls of the original building's grand staircase as it spirals up to the fifth floor. You'll also find yourself in the presence of some interesting art in Blakes, the modern upmarket restaurant named after the doyen of Beatles art Sir Peter Blake – the pop artist responsible for the 'Sgt Pepper's Lonely Hearts Club Band' album cover.

But the hotel is not awash with Beatlemania. Instead, the Hard Days Night manages a balancing act of paying the city's musical heroes rightful tribute while also catering to those who require top-class accommodation. And this is where the hotel bucks the themed-hotel stereotype. As well as placing The Beatles at the core of its existence, it is also adept in providing first-rate hospitality in a hotel that has been crafted to accommodate an aura of laidback cool with splashes of opulence

for instance, the building's original marble columns and central
aircase. Having mastered the art in the public areas, the hotel
xtends this approach to the other 110 rooms, which are just as
pscale and offer guests a modern and indulgent retreat.
longside the touches of lavishness there are also dashes of
himsical fun such as the funky yellow submarine jukebox that
ts in the lobby.

If the purpose of your stay is a weekend love-in, why not go
ie extra mile and get hitched at the hotel's 'Two of Us'
edding chapel? This shamelessly romantic setting (for any avid
eatles fan) can also accommodate wedding receptions for up to
50 guests.

Finally, take note: only ardent fans should stay here as the
otel doesn't just play Beatles music, it plays it 24/7. In short, to
ay here, you need more than love – you need infatuation.

lard Days Night Hotel, Central Buildings, 41 North John
treet, Liverpool L2 6RR, UK

44) 0151 236 1964
ww.harddaysnighthotel.com
quiries@harddaysnighthotel.com

SEE

ALBERT DOCK
Liverpool L3 4AA; www.albertdock.com
Head for the city's Albert Dock if you want to explore an area
packed with visitor attractions, restaurants and bars. Choose
between the expected Beatles Story or the more surprising
International Slavery Museum. For a taste of the supernatural, take
a guided walk with Shiverpool Ghost Tours. And if all that culture
becomes too much, plonk yourself down at any one of a great
selection of bars and restaurants nearby.

BEATLES MAGICAL MYSTERY TOUR
www.beatlestour.org

What better way to explore The Beatles' old hunting ground than from a seat on a colourful bus resembling the one in The Beatles' *Magical Mystery Tour*? You'll visit places that soon became landmarks after being referenced in Beatles songs ('Penny Lane', 'Strawberry Fields') childhood homes and schools, and the mop-tops', before ending at the famous Cavern Club.

BE SEEN

THE CASBAH COFFEE CLUB
8 Haymans Green, West Derby, Liverpool L12 7JG;
www.casbahcoffeeclub.com

Known simply as 'the Casbah', this venue's history has warranted its status as a Grade II-listed building. Opened in 1959 by Mona Best – mother of original Beatles drummer Pete Best – the Casbah's decor remains unchanged since The Quarrymen painted it and then rocked its tiny stage. It is the only Beatles venue to be preserved in its original guise, making it a must-visit for Beatles fans.

NEWZ BAR
18 Water Street, Liverpool L2 8TD; www.newzbar.co.uk

Revamped with red leather booths and lanterns and with one of the longest bars in Europe, Newz Bar is one of Liverpool's top nightspots. For rock 'n' roll-star treatment, reserve a booth and a hostess will serve you and your gang all night long. With the red-carpeted entrance, it's impossible not to feel like a celebrity; indeed, a few will be spotted.

THE PORTOBELLO

~~·◊%%◊·~~

The Portobello acquired its own peculiar mythology by way of a baronial rock star, a cinematic icon, a high-fashion model, and a plethora of pop stars, rock stars, Britpop stars… Oh, and a couple of goths, too. George Michael and the gravelly-voiced Tina Turner are among the pop stars to have checked in, while goths Siouxsie and the Banshees and Marc Almond maintained their ghostly pallor hiding out at The Portobello's hotel bar, and, in 1988, former Britpopper Damon Albarn worked behind it (he once remarked that Bono was rude to him and that he has 'never really forgiven him' but that the Edge 'was always really polite'.)

The Portobello, like many a rock 'n' roll hotel, also has its affiliations with rock 'n' roll's drug-induced woes. In 1980, unwieldy cult rocker/acid casualty Roky Erickson conducted an interview with famous *NME* scribe Nick Kent in which Roky only managed to confirm his avalanche slide into madness by offering long pauses and blank looks before declaring that he was 'the devil's chosen one'. The interview had to be conducted over a two-day period at the hotel, as Roky's brain appeared to keep short-circuiting, offering little in the way of conversation. Fittingly, Kent titled the journalistic piece 'I Talked with a Zombie'.

Also enshrined in 'Portobello legend' is the tale of Alice Cooper requesting deliveries of white mice for the boa constrictor he was keeping in his room; apparently, the local pet shop duly obliged.

Although it's located in London's characterful Notting Hill, you'd be forgiven for walking straight past The Portobello. Only the two planters, placed strategically either side of the entrance, signal it out as a hotel, as it sits alongside the other houses of an inconspicuous but rather grand terrace. However, once inside, the story is altogether different. Just 24 rooms make up this exclusive retreat, and each one evinces the possibility of unbridled indulgence. A variety of furnishings is on display across the rooms, exuding elegant character from every corner. In one of the rooms you'll find an Elizabethan four-poster bed so large a set of steps have been provided so that guests can climb in easily. Elsewhere, Moroccan chambers of mahogany and red tapestries are complemented with gilt mirrors and birdcages. And for the real swashbuckler, there's the Colonial Room, which comes with a sunken jacuzzi. The classic vintage room, however, is the Round Room: a large round canopied bed flanked by Edwardian decor, provides an air of serenity and discretion. And then there's the lobby, with red velvet couches so comfy that lingering is positively encouraged.

Yet, despite its multifarious styles, The Portobello manages to remain typically English. Maybe it's the rose garden (enjoyed by most of the rooms), the Victorian chairs tucked away in corners or just the supercilious Kensington location, but the hotel feels both Victorian and hip. It is almost as though The Portobello is at the intersection of the decadent world of rock music and the romantic ideals of Lord Byron. With this in mind, it is no surprise that The Portobello was voted as having the 'sexiest beds' by *Harpers & Queen*. Indeed, this hotel is best suited for those who wish to have a few luxurious nights with a special someone to display their amorous inclinations. Which is exactly what the aforementioned cinematic icon (Johnny Depp) and the high-fashion model (Kate Moss) decided to do when they checked into The Portobello. While ensconced in this swanky hideaway, the dazzling duo enjoyed a champagne bath to display their affection. And who can blame them? A freestanding claw-foot bath, embellished with numerous Victorian nozzles, is surely more suited to a night of decadent trysts than a quick solitary dip.

The Portobello doesn't have an onsite restaurant, but the equally famous Julie's Restaurant and Bar is just around the corner on Portland Road. Named after its owner – Julie Hodges – the restaurant conveys the same finesse as the hotel's cultivated rooms, since Julie handled the interior design for both establishments. So, expect the same dazzling mix of themes, designed to suit your every mood, in the grand but intimate restaurant; hotel guests are given a 10 per cent discount at Julie's.

Another great facet of The Portobello is its discreet service. You won't have conspicuous staff trying to pre-empt your every whim but, with 24-hour room service, they're always there if needed. And with a service like that, it's easy to see why the hotel has bewitched a procession of celebrities, including Van Morrison and Tina Turner. In fact, Tina Turner was so taken with The Portobello and its environs, she bought the house next door.

The Portobello Hotel, 22 Stanley Gardens, London W11 2NG, UK

+44) 020 7727 2777
info@portobellohotel.com
www.portobellohotel.com

SEE

CAMDEN MARKETS
Camden, London; www.camdenlock.net
For the best and biggest range of alternative, goth and vintage clothing fit for rock stars, head north to Camden for a browse around the markets; the place is positively bustling at the weekends. And if you come over all Kat Von D, then pop into one of the many tattoo and body-piercing parlours. As you amble around, you'll spot the many local independent record and bookshops.

MUSEUM OF BRANDS, PACKAGING AND ADVERTISING
2 Colville Mews, Lonsdale Road, London W11 2AR; www.museumofbrands.com
For a completely contrasting experience, take a trip down memory lane and find out how the image and marketing of your favourite teen magazines, sweets and groceries have evolved.

BE SEEN

THE COBDEN CLUB
170 Kensal Road, London W10 5BN; www.cobdenclub.co.uk
A luxurious private members club offering live theatre, burlesque and music. Guests at The Portobello receive a complimentary evening membership. The club occupies three floors featuring a minimalist bar on the ground floor, an opulent cocktail bar on the first floor and a spacious bar not unlike a ballroom at the top of the building. The Cobden is also known as the place to see new bands.

THE LONSDALE
48 Lonsdale Road, London W11 2DE; www.thelonsdale.co.uk
A lounge-restaurant and award-winning cocktail bar, the Lonsdale serves up delicious food, music and magic tricks. At weekends, the relaxed atmosphere is transformed as DJs crank up the volume and the front bar becomes a dancefloor.

K WEST

It perhaps goes without saying that today's rock 'n' roll-star hopefuls have to be more business-savvy bon-vivant than defenestrating delinquent in order to make it in the music business of the 21st Century.

In an age where music is compressed, downloaded and shared to the point of complete ubiquity, it would appear that 21st-century musicians need to be au fait with the unremitting pace of music's relationship with technological (r)evolution. Longer tours as a means to compensate for nominal royalties that trickle through from CD sales are also a necessity today, if The Next Big Thing wants to avoid returning to his Tesco day job.

As a result, musicians are adopting an enterprising approach to rock 'n' roll living – an approach that dispenses with that hedonistic pastime of turning hotel rooms into scenes from Sodom and Gomorrah in favour of bedding down in comfy hotels with fluffy pillows. Within these sanctuaries, their hosts' priority is to pander to every whimsical need rather than simply turn a blind eye to the egregious rock star swinging from the chandelier (if you just want to read about those kind of shenanigans, turn to the Comfort Inn Downtown on page 21). Yep, chances are that today's rock stars don't see windows as escape routes for TVs, preferring them soundproofed and with blackout blinds. Evidently, catering to this new generation of hard-touring acts requires the utmost in judicious hospitality skills.

Stepping into the breach is the deliciously hip K West Hotel & Spa. Employing a 'music and entertainment sales director' to ensure its jet-setting guests' expectations are met, K West makes sure that not only do today's rock stars have their privacy protected but also that all the bands' hors d'œuvre are served according to their tastes and the spa heated just so.

And it seems to be working, too.

News of K West's attentive service has spread fast throughout the cadre of tour managers and booking agents. On any given day, one can find any number of doe-eyed musicians in all their shabby glamour dawdling through the chic lobby, such is the hotel's increasing popularity in rock 'n' roll circles. Among those who rank on rock 'n' roll's cooler-than-thou list: American troubadour Josh Ritter was spotted lugging a tour-worn guitar case through the hotel, while members from Courtney Love's Hole were slumping into chairs in reception. After appearing on *I'm a Celebrity...* , loveable rogue Shaun Ryder sat sipping a Red Bull at K West as he informed a journalist from influential music rag *NME* of the best ways to navigate the perilous road to rock-star fame (incidentally, his sage advice included getting your dad to do your soundchecks and ignoring record producers when recording your albums).

If all this talk of rock stars simply lounging about reception ha made the state of contemporary rock 'n' roll hotels sound a little *too* soporific, well, fear not. Just because there's no chandelier-swingin or ragged rockers ODing with call girls in their beds, it doesn't mean that K West is devoid of a party atmosphere. For a start, the cosy K Lounge keeps the records spinning until the early hours for those looking to groove with a suave crowd. However, more enticingly, the bands have been known to bring the party to the hotel. After the 2006 NME Awards, Arctic Monkeys partied with other NME darlings – such as Editors and We Are Scientists – at K West, where the likes of Kelly Osbourne and Carl Barat were als enjoying an aftershow soiree. Indeed, K West's hushed corridors can suddenly be awakened by a band and their entourage checking in at any hour. To that end, K West is quickly establishing itself as *the* hotel in London in which you can pull up a bar stool and find yourself seated among the buzz bands of the day.

From the outset this might all seem too affectedly exclusive, but K West has not forgotten that it needs to dote on all its guests. With this is mind, the hotel offers the chance for guests who live outside – as Spinal Tap put it – 'the majesty of rock and the fantasy of roll' to quit the ordinary life and experience what it's like in the rock-star realm by offering a 'Rock 'n' Roll Package' that includes a 3-hour recording session, accommodation in an Executive room and a full English breakfast. And you can add a bottle of champagne for a mere £40. The recording sessions take place at the boutique recording studio just round the corner from the hotel. The fully equipped, swish studio has been used by many a professional warbler, including Robbie Williams, Stevie Wonder and Adele.

If the studio doesn't sway you, then the Executive room certainly will: a spacious haven of understated elegance with the standard fare of TV, CD/DVD player and mp3 player included, it is a room that emanates a sense of calm that belies the bustle of the bar below. Though if you want to go all out and live the dream, then opt for the cutting-edge K Suite, whose glass walls separate the living room and bedroom and oversized showers; staying in this room is like living in a high-end New York apartment.

So what of the spa? Well, as you might expect, it will sate the appetite of anyone in pursuit of luxury. Consequently, the hotel's facilities don't fall under the celebs' radar either – Dizzee Rascal has been seen unwinding in the sauna. No doubt after a long night of going 'Bonkers'.

K West Hotel & Spa, Richmond Way, London W14 0AX, UK
+44) 020 8008 6600
ookit@k-west.co.uk
www.k-west.co.uk

SEE

GINGLIK
1 Shepherds Bush Green, London W12 8PH; www.ginglik.co.uk
Okay, it may be housed in a former public toilet but this underground club, located just 5 minutes' walk from K West, is a hidden gem. With music, comedy nights and movie nights, this funky club has a packed diary. Plus, you never know who's going to take to the stage: Robin Williams once made his way through the unprepossessing entrance to perform a surprise set at the club.

NOTTING HILL ARTS CLUB
21 Notting Hill Gate, Notting Hill, London W11 3JQ;
www.nottinghillartsclub.com
The circular bar in this venue is regularly packed with West London's unutterably cool crowd. And rightly so, too. This venue has its finger on the pulse when it comes to the buzz bands of the day. Of course, the surfeit of groups coming through the club's door probably has something to do with the fact that Alan McGee (the former head honcho of Creation Records, responsible for giving the world Oasis) runs his Death Disco night here.

BE SEEN

BABYLON AT THE ROOF GARDENS
99 Kensington High Street, London W8 5SA; www.roofgardens.com
So you've been schmoozing with the funky young crowd at K West, now all that's left is to wine and dine somewhere equally vibrant and chic. Head over to Richard Branson's rooftop gardens and you'll be treated to spectacular views from the Babylon restaurant on the seventh floor, where glitz, cocktails and sumptuous food come together to form a glamorous haven a hundred feet above the city.

WESTBOURNE HOUSE
65 Westbourne Grove, London W2 4UJ; www.westbournehouse.net
Keeping with the elegant touches, this cocktail bar caters to a swanky crowd with an equally swanky cocktail menu. Classy but cool.

PAVILION

————— ✦26✦ —————

Pete Doherty is on a tawdry-looking bed, planting a kiss on a man who is of equally unkempt appearance. Jarvis Cocker, perched on a floral footstool, leans forward as if to whisper something of utmost secrecy. And James Dean Bradfield, lead vocalist with Manic Street Preachers, hardly seems fazed by the fact that he is seated in a room awash with leopard-skin prints and pink tassels, surrounded by a bevy of beauties collectively known as the Sugababes. Elsewhere, Brian Ferry is looking forlorn as he stares into the camera lens surrounded by a coterie of models amid the kaleidoscopic colours of the Afro Room. Meanwhile, singer Bebel Gilberto appears to be sharing a joke with pianist Jools Holland in the hotel's lounge, otherwise known as The Burgundy Parlour – a name which goes some way to displaying the flamboyant level of thinking behind this formerly drab hotel.

After reading the intro, you'd be forgiven for thinking that this bordello hosted the love-in of love-ins reserved only for rock stars. But truth be told, the Pavilion is merely the perfect backdrop for stylists of music and fashion photographic shoots. The hotel's gaudy decor has to be seen to be believed but, in the meantime, think oversized prop cupboard of all that is chintzy. The Enter the Dragon room, for instance, is like a child's jewellery box overspilling with faux gold and silk cloth. Elsewhere, it's like going to stay with an old aunt who, with coiffured bouffant held aloft, struts about a home filled with everything that caught her magpie eye, wears a leopard-print nightgown all day and believes she still looks like a young Rita Hayworth. It will come as no surprise, then, that the hotel was opened by a former fashion model and his sister, who were tired

135

of the 'boring hotels around the world'. And so the two siblings put their creative heads together to open up their imaginations to the world in the form of this hotel.

Suffice to say, for the fastidious luxury hotel addict it may all prove a little too quirky as eccentric decors vie for space in cramped corners. On the other hand, if you like your hotel to be a feast for the eyes, then the Pavilion will prove to be the apogee of bohemian brilliance. Indeed, there have been many a creative-type for whom the gaudiness has equalled glamour: Ian Brown, Neneh Cherry, Feeder, Daft Punk, Badly Drawn Boy, Faithless and even Californian surfers The Beach Boys have all stepped into the cultivated clutter of the Pavilion.

So, it's a bit overwrought and fussy but at the same time it's incredibly good fun. Besides, where else could you stay and say Naomi Campbell was in your room flanked by two naked women in bondage gear? (In a photo shoot, that is.)

Pavilion Hotel, 34–36 Sussex Gardens, London W2 1UL, UK
(+44) 020 7262 0905
info@pavilionhoteluk.com
www.pavilionhoteluk.com

SEE

CAMDEN CRAWL
Camden Town; www.thecamdencrawl.com
As the name suggests, this multivenue festival takes place all over Camden Town. Each year, 200 bands raid the North London district to play to discerning music fans over the course of a weekend in early May. Spread over a mile and a half, and across 40 venues, the Crawl delivers top-name acts alongside those making (experimental) noises on the underground. As well as the live music, the Crawl also hosts comedy, theatre, short films and visual art.

BRICK LANE CURRY FESTIVAL

Brick Lane; www.bricklanecurryfestival.com

East London's Brick Lane is home to a two-week cornucopia of curry tasting. The finale peaks at the Vibe Bar, where visitors can sample a shortlist of curries and vote for the Best Curry on Brick Lane. To add some authentic Indian touches, there are Bollywood dancers, snake-charmers and live music sessions with the likes of Bobby Friction.

BE SEEN

CROBAR

17 Manette Street, London W1D 4AS; www.crobar.co.uk

A bar dedicated to bourbon, beer and rock music, the Crobar is a regular haunt for local rock bands, music journalists and the odd record company executive or two. Among those who have dropped in for a tipple include: Dave Grohl, Slash and Alice Cooper. Running the gamut of rock, from John Lee Hooker to latter-day metal bands, the Crobar's jukebox is more of a comprehensive guide to rock music than any anthology you'll ever read. In fact, the Crobar is so rockin' it even released its own compilation album.

BARFLY

19 Chalk Farm Road, Camden, London NW1 8AN;
www.barflyclub.com

Visit the Barfly for the best in up-and-coming bands. This intimate live music venue showcases bands every night of the week. Rub shoulders with record execs checking out the stars of tomorrow.

SANCTUM SOHO

~~◦✕℞◦~~

Metallica's Kirk Hammett once remarked that he wrote the classic 'Enter Sandman' riff at 3a.m. thrashing at his guitar in his hotel room. No doubt many a budding rock star, or anyone with a reverence for rock 'n' roll hedonism, would love to experience such a raucous antic... Well, at Sanctum Soho, you can. In fact, you don't even need to have your own guitar – you can hire one from reception.

Professing to be 'London's first rock 'n' roll boutique hotel', Sanctum Soho is the brainchild of nightclub owner and entrepreneur Mark Fuller, who earned his rock 'n' roll chips touring with the likes of Thin Lizzy and The Damned. And the credentials don't stop there: Iron Maiden's management are investors and, as seen on the BBC documentary *Rock 'n' Roll Hotel*, Maiden's drummer, Nicko McBrain, road-tested one of the open-plan Junior Suites.

Set within two converted Georgian townhouses, this hideaway for rock stars comprises of just 30 rooms and is situated in London's convivial and fashionable West End. The rooms are individually themed and sumptuously furnished, creating perfect havens for those who are disdainful of the predictable. The Crash Pads, as the name suggests, are designed for those just looking to crash for the night and convalesce following an evening of nocturnal pursuits. (Incidentally, guests at the Sanctum gain free entry into Mark Fuller's other venture, the Embassy nightclub in nearby Mayfair.)

At the other end of the scale, the Two-Bedroom Garden Loft Suite, with two freestanding baths, dressing areas, spacious terrace and a decor flecked with smouldering reds and chocolate browns, would suit any A-list celebrity looking for a home from

139

home. The delectable open-plan Junior Suite is a magnet for the permissive as it features a freestanding bath, visible from sleeping and seating areas, while the rest of the room appears to be enshrouded in glass and silver. Elsewhere, there are Parisian-style Loft Suites oozing bohemian chic, Superior Suites exhibiting rococo fantasy and an elegantly styled Balcony Suite with a circular bed.

All rooms come with Wii console, iPod dock, Internet access and a 'box of tricks', which has been known to include a pair of Myla knickers and a sex kit. However, for any touring rock star, the hotel's crowning glory is the rooftop garden with its 24-hour bar and hot tub. And for those who are really unapologetic about worshipping at the altar of rock 'n' roll, you can also hire a Harley Davidson and rumble around the West End in true 'hog' style. Though don't expect to be able to ride down the hotel's hallways; the Sanctum's impresarios are keen to stress that they don't want the place left looking as though Keith Moon has stayed for a few nights. But if you want your bath filled with Jack Daniels, 'it can be arranged', promises owner Mark Fuller. And yet, despite the amenities and service on offer, you don't have to feel obliged to constantly indulge. For example, if you just want to relax, there are plenty of on-demand films to watch on your flat-screen TV or, if you prefer, take yourself off to enjoy one in the hotel's own cinema.

As you might expect from a hotel keen to draw on the glitz and glamour of the rock world's jet set, the front-desk staff are dressed in black, à la Elvis's Heartbreak Hotel (see page 81), and are available to attend to your every need 24 hours a day; this includes arranging in-room hair appointments, limousine hire and private security. You'll find that the front-desk attire suits the ambience of the ground floor wonderfully as you step out of the revolving doors at the entrance and across a sleek oak floor, into a swarthy lobby. It's a bit like stepping into the gothic chambers belonging to an aristocratic libertine.

Sanctum's 60-seat restaurant – No. 20 – is equally enchanting, albeit with a slightly more opulent feel, as the dark-veneer tables are offset with lashings of gold and red crocodile-skin upholstery. At the helm is Head Chef Gavin Austin, whose culinary delights are 'quintessentially British', which serves to remind us that Sanctum Soho is not entirely *Hollywood Babylon* and is not afraid to add a dash of home-grown charm to proceedings. Besides, wouldn't you consider a full English breakfast to be ambrosia after a night of debauchery?

Sanctum Soho, 20 Warwick Street, London W1B 5NF, UK
(+44) 020 7292 6100
info@sanctumsoho.com
www.sanctumsoho.com

SEE

OPEN-AIR THEATRE REGENT'S PARK
Inner Circle, Regent's Park, London NW1 4NR;
www.openairtheatre.org
In the heart of Regent's Park lies a verdant spot with amphitheatre-style seating, perfectly suited for some summery Shakespearean action or a screening of a cult film. From June to September, you can bring along your own picnic or grab some Pimms on the lawn. But as the English summer isn't always, well, summery, bring an extra layer for when the sun goes down.

NOTTING HILL CARNIVAL
Chepstow Road, Notting Hill, Westbourne Grove and Ladbroke Grove, London W11; www.thenottinghillcarnival.com
This colourful carnival, held every August Bank Holiday since 1966, is the largest of its kind in Europe. This isn't a venue-centred festival; revellers and costumed paraders fill the streets of Notting

Hill with music (read steel bands, reggae and sound systems) and dancing, and Caribbean foods stalls waft about wonderfully enticing smells. Sunday is the children's parade, with the main parade kicking off on the Monday.

BE SEEN

PUNK
14 Soho Street, Soho, London W1D 3DN; www.punksoho.co.uk
This Soho club, well known for celebrity-spotting, is a popular hangout for the likes of Kate Moss and Kelly Osbourne. The name is more an indication of attitude than music, and you'll find everything from cabaret to Rockaoke in what the promoters promise will be an 'unusual' experience. Decor includes bespoke colourful furniture and backlit honeycomb walls.

MADAME JOJO'S
8–10 Brewer Street, Soho, London W1F 0SE;
www.madamejojos.com
A stylish Soho club with new DJ music, numerous live events and kitsch cabaret, Madame Jojo's is still going strong after more than 50 years in business. The boudoir-style environment reflects the venue's previous life as a strip club. Enjoy a range of different themed nights in decadent and intimate surroundings.

HOTEL CENTRAL

Are you sitting comfortably? Then, we'll begin... with a lesson in the history of heavy metal. In the late 1980s, heavy metal assumed an altogether more satanic stance that pushed the boundaries to extremes – a push that would culminate in church burnings, suicide and murder by the mid 1990s. This nihilistic strand of heavy metal would come to be known as black metal.

Adopting a ghoulish appearance with the use of 'corpse paint', a small group of young bands in Norway – isolated in their own underworld of misanthropy and seething hatred – barked out their diatribes against Christianity and, well, everybody, over a cacophony of raw-sounding guitars played at breakneck speed. One of the first such bands to unleash this ferocious sound was Mayhem.

After a couple of rudimentary demos, Mayhem released a mini-album called 'Deathcrush' in 1987, which singled them out as progenitors of the black metal scene, before their vocalist, the portentously named 'Dead' (Per Yngve Ohlin, to his mum) blew his brains out with a shotgun in 1991. The band's guitarist Øystein Aarseth (aka Euronymous) was first on the blood-splattered scene. Proving his black metal, err, mettle, Øystein picked his way through the gory mess to collect pieces of skull, which he then used to decorate a necklace. Bristling with sordid ambition, the guitarist took a photo of 'Dead', aware of what such a picture would mean for his reputation among the rest of the black metal contingent. Øystein's next step in carving out his role as arbiter for this little circle of delinquent satanists was to open a record shop called Helvete (or Hell), which helped fund the releases on his record label Deathlike Silence

Productions (DSP) as well as provide a meeting place for those subscribing to satanic pretensions.

In this substrata of extreme music – once famous for being the genre in which its adherents were continually trying to outdo each other in the evil stakes – it was an almost predictable twist of fate that Mayhem's career would be plagued by death. In 1993, Øystein was murdered by Varg Vikernes, whose one-man band – Burzum – Øystein had signed to his DSP label.

Flash forward to November 2009. Mayhem members are staying at Hotel Central, somewhat perturbed by the fact they've been booked into double rooms instead of the requested singles. Sound too futile a problem for a band usually consumed with the penning of satanic mantras and taking pictures of their dead friends? Well, throw a dodgy promoter, who has run off with the money, into the mix and you can perhaps see why the band didn't much feel like spending the night in their rooms twiddling with their inverted crosses and wondering which subterranean antics in praise of Satan remained untapped. Besides, black metal has elevated itself above cult status since the early church-burning days and is now a viable commodity, attracting mainstream press for the quality of music as opposed to just the satanic lunacy that had once made the scene so ripe for mockery. So, it was only a matter of time before they started behaving badly and abandoned themselves to the time-honoured tradition of hotel trashing.

So, having been suitably antagonised by a covetous promoter, the Norwegian metallers and their crew recklessly coursed through their rooms: TVs and beds were destroyed, mirrors were smashed, curtains torn down, plants thrown out onto the street below, sinks demolished, blood spilt, walls stained and pipes burst. The band was arrested the following morning after a hotel employee entered one of the rooms and discovered the scene of devastation. However, it has to be said that while it is gratifying to have a recent addition to the rock 'n' roll pantheon of debauchery, it probably won't be considered to be on a par with Led Zeppelin's partying at the Riot House in LA (see page 57).

A dowdy-looking complex comprising of just 25 rooms, Hotel Central certainly isn't the Ritz. Needless to say, it is probably only Mayhem's notorious stay at the hotel that endows it with any modicum of fame. Yet despite being less than a sparkly abode, the hotel offers comfortable, modestly furnished rooms. Its strongest point, however, is the restaurant and bar area. Decorated chiefly with panelled wood, brass and muted colours, it has a style that recalls the roaring 20s. You get the feeling it is a style they've tried to achieve with the exterior. But, like a lot of art-deco buildings, it looks a little lost and outdated among its surroundings.

However, the real bugbear is that not all rooms have their own toilets. A fact that really pissed off Mayhem, apparently. Even satanists have to get up in the night to pee.

Hotel Central, Spoorlaan 422, 5038 CG Tilburg, The Netherlands

+31) 013 543 62 34
info@hotelcentraltilburg.nl
www.hotelcentraltilburg.nl

SEE

ROADBURN FESTIVAL
013 Poppodium, Veemarktstraat 44, 5038 CV Tilburg;
www.roadburn.com
A huge international and well-respected three-day music festival for headbangers. Expect every subgenre of heavy metal: doom, death metal, black metal and psychedelic. This underground festival puts

on some of the most interesting and exciting bands currently working the circuit. And yet, despite ear-bludgeoning sounds being emitted from the stage, this is a very friendly, laidback festival.

DE PONT FOUNDATION
Wilhelminapark 1, 5041 EA Tilburg; www.depont.nl
De Pont museum of contemporary art is a light-filled and cool place to chill out. Bask in its calming atmosphere before checking out its latest exhibitions and well-stocked café. Its permanent collection includes modern art from Alberola to Zandvliet, with others such as Anish Kapoor and Bill Viola thrown in for good measure.

BE SEEN

013
Veemarktstraat 44, 5038 CV Tilburg; www.013.nl
If you're not in Tilburg at the time of the Roadburn festival, you can still get a healthy dose of heavy metal at the Metal Matinee, which also takes place at 013. This unique metallic venue is a hub of creativity. Aside from hosting international acts, it also has a smaller venue – the Bat Cave – which is home to the more avant-garde performer and boasts a studio and several rehearsal rooms. From the moment you arrive at 013, you know you're in for something special: the venue's facade is cloaked in shimmering CDs and black rubber. Sounds tacky but looks amazing.

LITTLE DEVIL
Stationsstraat 27, 5038 EA Tilburg; www.littledevil.nl
Rawk 'n' Roll Café Little Devil has a schedule packed with live music (death metal, indie, punk) as well as club nights (such as Classic Hardrock), darts tournaments, whisky-tasting sessions and pub quizzes. In case you forget the name of the pub, it's decorated throughout in red and black with skeletons dangling from the ceiling.

BACKSTAGE HOTEL

Last night's gig at the Paradiso (or was it the Melkweg?) is still ringing in your ears. As you wake, you feel the all-consuming hangover kick in. Peeling your head from the pillow, you notice a drummer's stool, the luminous glow of make-up lights and the oil-slick sheen of flightcases. Baffled, you try to croak a cursory 'what the…?' but your voice is burnt to a sandpapered rasp. Whichever venue you were at, you'll be convinced you've been stowed away in a backstage area with the entire band's gear. But when you finally come round, you'll see that you weren't far off with your dreary-eyed assumption: this hotel isn't far from the backstage areas of either venue.

It's easy to see why the decor inside the BackStage Hotel may confound and confuse those who spend the majority of their days on the road. Hallmarked by flightcase furniture and stage spotlights, the hotel has been designed to house touring bands in familiar surroundings. Although the hotel is evidently resolute in its attempts to be rock 'n' roll, it is not merely a novelty hotel; yes, there's the album artwork and the snare-drum light-fittings, showcasing an effusive playfulness (further exemplified by offers of air-guitar rental and ski storage), but the real coup here is the service: they have extended breakfast hours, free laundry service, room to store equipment and the staff are eminently helpful – they've even been known to take on the role of roadies.

Indeed, it's an approach that is earning the hotel considerable interest from errant road hogs; even veteran rockers Status Quo wanted to book 26 rooms; unfortunately, the hotel has only 22. Bands concerned with levels of privacy may be impressed to learn that the BackStage Hotel promises to remain tight-lipped about who's sleeping beneath the glare of the spotlights that hang above the beds. Those wishing to prise a coveted guestbook from the hotel's grasp will have to make do with trying to decipher the autographs scrawled onto the piano, which sits in the 24-hour private bar. Although don't expect the names of many stadium rockers to be etched around the ivories. This two-star hotel probably falls beneath the radar for those with five-star appetites, gargantuan tour buses and bloated egos, though, that said, you will find the names of credible acts such as Fleet Foxes, TV on the Radio, The Errors, Cage the Elephant, and ex-Libertines frontman Carl Barat, scribbled onto the aforementioned piano.

If, however, your tour is not being bankrolled by a major label haemorrhaging money, then this is the place to crash when you're in Amsterdam. Not that this is a seedy 'I can see my neighbours through the holes in the wall' type of place. On the contrary, the rooms are slick, minimalist and comfortable, with the bare essentials: a TV and an iPod docking station. Still, you may want to make a note of the fact that only the Quad Rooms and the Five-Person Rooms have their own bathrooms. Those staying in all other room types have to use the shared showers and toilets in the corridor.

Despite the low-budget environs, the BackStage Hotel pulls a further masterstroke with the lobby area. These confined quarters, mired in rock 'n' roll paraphernalia, greet you with a Heineken Welcome Pack, a game of pool and a pledge to indoctrinate you in the ways of the road. Every inch the rock 'n' roll bar, this is, you sense, the preferred watering hole for unshaven, dishevelled roadies intent on lifting beer after beer rather than amp after amp.

Amsterdam may not be the liberal haven it once was, but a bit of counterculture still thrives in this enclave. It's refreshing to see the hotel staff do away with stuffy uniforms and dress instead in their own attire. It feels more personal and friendly, which is why a network of international touring bands returns to the BackStage Hotel time and time again. Plus, with all the music venues in the locale, it's not surprising that a hotel of this nature has sprung up.

The hotel's MySpace site states that they would like to meet 'record companies who still press vinyl records, journalists who do original interviews and roadies without back problems'. But if you're not in the music biz, there's no need to feel sidelined as they also would like to meet 'music-minded people without headphones' and 'experienced travellers with big feet'.

BackStage Hotel, Leidsegracht 114, 1016 CT Amsterdam, The Netherlands

(+31) 020 624 40 44
info@backstagehotel.com
www.backstagehotel.com

SEE

MELKWEG
Lijnbaansgracht 234a, 1017 PH Amsterdam; www.melkweg.nl
A fantastic venue almost a plectrum's throw from the hotel, the Melkweg (Milky Way) has been run by a non-profit organisation since the 1970s. This collection of art spaces hosts live music, theatre, photography and multimedia exhibitions; the club has three stages under one roof. It also hosts a cannabis festival every November.

PARADISO
Weteringschans 6–8, 1017 SG Amsterdam; www.paradiso.nl
This former church has great acoustics and an impressive list of bands that have played here. The eclectic programme runs the gamut of music from rock (The Rolling Stones, Prince and the Sex Pistols) to classical. This venue has gained iconic status and is the best-known in town.

BE SEEN

CAFÉ DE KOE
Marnixstraat 381, 1016 XR Amsterdam; www.cafedekoe.nl
If you fancy a game of pool with some local musos, head to this cosy and unpretentious place. With fine food, beer and wine just a few steps from the hotel, this is the perfect chill-out pad. Cow Café features artwork and decor on a bovine theme.

HENK SCHIFFMACHER
Ceintuurbaan 416, 1074 EA Amsterdam; www.henkschiffmacher.nl
Pay a visit to Amsterdam's most famous tattoo artist at his parlour or check out what exhibitions Henk has been organising for the Maritime or Antiquities museums. Kurt Cobain, Red Hot Chili Peppers, Robbie Williams and Pamela Anderson all feature in Henk's client list, so rest assured you will be in safe and much sought-after hands.

KEMPINSKI BRISTOL

nown as 'the Kempi', this hotel on the prominent avenue of
urfürstendamm has long been extolled by the glitterati since
routing its first flashes of luxury from the humdrum of a
ost-war Berlin. Of course, over the years this edifying city has
come something of a cultural hotbed, spurring on the
velopment of more hotels. But rather than see its popularity
vindle amid the frisson of chi-chi accommodation, the Kempi
is yet to have its luxury crown usurped by any competition
d, consequently, still ranks high in the rock 'n' roll hierarchy. It
oves to be the sought-after stay for perennial touring
usicians when they hit the German tour circuit, with many
turning here to climb the red carpet at the entrance to be
elcomed by savvy staff into the hotel's old-world glamour.

The Kempi has what could be the world's most illustrious
iestbook: performers, musicians and even an actor-cum-
esident have left wistful goodbyes and notes of hearty
preciation within the pages of this bound tome. Flicking
rough its pages, you get a feel for why the guests return time
id time again.

Native punk-rockers Die Toten Hosen stated that the hotel
is 'as always, terribly nice' in 2005; Status Quo and Melanie C
ere equally courteous in expressing their gratitude, both of
em thanking the Kempi 'for a lovely stay' and Kelly Osbourne
clied the impudent reputation that helped her to prominence in
he Osbournes reality TV show, by simply stating that the hotel
is 'a wonderful place'. Yoko Ono, meanwhile, proved that she
is still holding on to the dream by writing 'imagine peace' in
006 and the mild-mannered Ronan Keating didn't defy
pectation with the cordial 'All the best and thanks for

everything'. As you can imagine, everyone's favourite pop-funksters Red Hot Chili Peppers 'had a great time', while the Pet Shop Boys and Jack Johnson made light of the great hospitality that has also managed to seduce the likes of Alice Cooper, Paul Weller and the infamous filmmaker Roman Polanski, the latter stating that it 'was nice to be back' in 2006 (no doubt, for the last time).

Not all of the Kempi's patrons are from musical spheres, however, and noted actors, directors and fashion designers (Christian Dior, for instance) have checked in at the hotel's gold and marble reception area. And when you're the type of hotel that can offer a Presidential Suite (the biggest in Berlin) that comprises five bedrooms, seven bathrooms and two living rooms across two floors, you herald a distinguished clientele that includes everyone from Ronald Reagan to the Dalai Lama.

Unsurprisingly, perhaps, given their profession, it is the actresses who make some of the more dramatic comments. Turning back the decades to 1966, German actress Brigitte Horney was compelled to write that it had been '… a celebration to be here'. And returning to the present, actress Saskia Vester declared that 'Berlin without my Kempi is like Paris without the Eiffel Tower'. Quite the accolade, you might say, but for all its mawkishness, there is truth to be had. The Kempi, with its grand exterior, exudes an air of romanticism as soon as you step inside. There might be a whiff of the haughty, but that's part of its traditional charm – a charm that has made it something of a landmark and as famous as the guests it houses. For years to come, many a rock star will be paraphrasing the guestbook entry made by actress Grete Weiser in 1952: 'The Kempinski is more beautiful than ever – the same cannot be said for me.' However, it's not only gushing praise that fills the pages of this illustrious guestbook: Chuck Berry concluded his stay, cryptically, by simply writing the word 'cheese'. Erm, cheers, Chuck.

Kempinski Hotel Bristol, Kurfürstendamm 27, 10719 Berlin, Germany

(+49) 03088 4340
reservations.bristol@kempinski.com
www.kempinski-berlin.de

SEE

KART BAHN
Karl-Friedrich-Benz-Strasse 2, 17268 Templin/Uckermark; www.kart-templin.de
Take a break from the city's cultural centre and race like a madman or madwoman around a track in a pocket Formula One car (in reverse on Wednesdays), then take a trip north out of Berlin to Uckermark. After you've broken all the records, take a pit stop in the F1 Restaurant to refuel on some hearty German fare.

BERLINER TRÖDELMARKT
Strasse des 17 Juni, 10623 Berlin; www.berliner-troedelmarkt.de
So you've spent all your money in the fine restaurants and bars along Kurfürstendamm but you want to buy a little something to take back home. Well, head to this market (a favourite among Berliners) on a Saturday or Sunday and you've every chance of picking up some unique clothing and a few interesting antiques. Haggling is positively encouraged.

BE SEEN

SO36
Oranienstrasse 190, 10999 Berlin; so36.de
Taking its name from the pre-World War II postal code of the area, this popular venue is one of the city's less conventional clubs. With a history of punk rock, SO36 has hosted Black Flag, Toy Dolls and

the Dead Kennedys. You'll now find everything from house club nights to hard-rock gigs, karaoke and a Turkish drag act.

FUSION FESTIVAL
17248 Lärz; www.fusion-festival.de

An hour and a half's drive out of Berlin takes you to Lärz – home of this unique independent festival, which grows in stature with each passing year. Taking place in June at an old Russian military airfield, its tickets (upwards of 50,000) often sell out at the beginning of each year before the acts have even been announced. That's the kind of adulation that this festival, which avoids corporate sponsorship and puts on theatre performances as well as music running the gamut of genres, attracts. You'll think that the carni' has rolled into town. There's no room for light sleepers either – music can be heard 24/7 over the festival's four days.

ADLON KEMPINSKI

Quite why anyone would want to dangle their child from a third-floor window with a blanket covering its head is beyond the comprehension of many. But then Michael Jackson was always a little outré, to say the least.

Maybe Jacko just got caught up in the ebullient commotion of it all. There was certainly a lot to be excitable about – the paparazzi, the maniacal crowd vying for a glimpse of his son, and the spectacular view of Berlin's famous former city gate – but one would have thought that the neutral hues and haughty refinement of the Presidential Suite would have calmed the Peter Pan Pop Star. It's no Neverland, after all.

This sense of understated charm pervades throughout. Even in places where you expect to find the tasselled, gilded and gaudy finishes in a top five-star hotel – such as the lobby, for example – you find chaste upholstery, unadorned arches, and muted colours.

But this is all to the Adlon's credit. It is not out to rival other hotels of similar stature; it has its own unique history from which to draw its inspiration – which is exactly what it did for its multimillion Euro renovation. Restoring the classic ambience of its glory days, the Adlon manages to overwhelm without ambushing you at every turn with ostentation. No wonder the rock stars are being drawn here. However, it must be said that this is a place for tea and scones as opposed to uppers and downers. In short, it's the sort of place that rock bands check into once they've started playing it safe. U2 have stayed here.

Hotel Adlon Kempinski, Unter den Linden 77, 10117 Berlin, Germany

(+49) 030 2261 1111
hotel.adlon@kempinski.com
www.hotel–adlon.de

SEE

FRITZ MUSIC TOURS
Schreinerstrasse 12, Berlin; www.musictours-berlin.com
Hit the streets of Berlin for a guided tour of its rock history, which includes entrance to the Ramones museum, or on a tour of the famous Hansa Studios. During his three years in Berlin in the 1970s, David Bowie recorded here as well as producing tracks for Iggy Pop. Still in use today, the studio is popular with bands such as Snow Patrol and Green Day.

SAGE CLUB
Köpenicker Strasse 76, 10179 Berlin; www.sage-club.de
One of Berlin's oldest clubs, Sage has lost not one iota of its allure for a young crowd looking to rock out to bands and DJs in a unique setting. While strange fantastical gargoyles watch over the bar, gigs, aftershow catwalk parties and album launch parties take place across a number of floors in a labyrinthine club that's topped off with a swimming pool in the lounge area (though you're not actually allowed in the pool).

BE SEEN

KNAACK KLUB
Greifswalder Strasse 224, 10245 Berlin; www.knaack-berlin.de
On the musical menu there's everything from high-energised rock to the more chilled ambience evoked by jazz-orientated acts. It is a diversity that permeates the whole club, which is spread over four floors: there's the live music venue (with an average of about four gigs a week through a mix of German and international acts), the Dizzy Lounge (a plush room that hosts karaoke nights and features a billiards table) and two floors of dancing space. The dark, narrow

entry way would have you believe that this is a bit of a dive, but in fact it's a swanky place that attracts the high priests of hip.

ROCK 'N' ROLL HERBERGE
Muskauer Strasse 11, 10997 Berlin; www.rock-n-roll-herberge.de
So, you're in Berlin for a few days but you haven't released your own 'Thriller' to finance a stay at the Adlon. For a more low-key rock 'n' roll stay, try this hostel 'by musicians for musicians' (and for Keith Moon copyists, given that the rooms feature 'indestructible beds'). The basement bar is a punk-rocker, late-night drinker-friendly watering hole. Not that you need to descend to the subterranean drinking den to know this. The hostel's statement of intent is made clear from the off with the faces of AC/DC's Bon Scott and The Clash's Joe Strummer adorning the exterior. Even if you're not checking in here, head over for their midweek cocktail party to mix and chat with like-minded free spirits.

WESTIN EXCELSIOR ROME

A great deal of praise has been heaped upon the Excelsior; such is its flair for evoking feelings of prestige for all guests who climb the red-carpeted steps to pass through its grand entrance. The Excelsior has won the affection of not only luxury-travel writers (it featured in *Condé Nast Traveller*'s 2006 Gold List) but also the hearts of rock stars, movie stars and statesmen.

Its popularity among the cognoscenti was initially fuelled by its connection to Federico Fellini's 1960 film *La Dolce Vita*, by dint of the hotel sitting in the area around the Via Veneto that features prominently in the film. It's an apt union as Fellini's bewitching style perfectly conveyed the atmosphere of the Excelsior – the beautiful people gesticulating in sumptuous surroundings, enjoying the unremitting celebrity parties that were continually in full swing: American film producer Joseph E. Levine threw parties in his suite, which ended with spaghetti on the crystal chandeliers, while Ava Gardner and Frank Sinatra played out their tempestuous marriage here, to the bemusement of Excelsior guests and staff. But not all were afforded such servile service, as a head barman once remarked: 'I once politely asked a member of The Rolling Stones to wear something more suitable than shorts to the bar, only for him to return in long trousers sporting a very, very interesting, "design". The barman in question concluded it would have been wiser to have left the Stone in his shorts well alone.

As the decades passed, the number of screen sirens, iconic crooners and lovelorn hangers-on dwindled, and the Excelsior had time to recuperate, somewhat, after the broiling times experienced in *La Dolce Vita's* era. But, the most famous guest to have stayed at the Excelsior is someone whose visit is not that widely reported, at least, not by the hotel (no doubt due to consternation over being associated with a dissipated act of excess). If you're an avid reader of the music press, then you'll already know what is coming next... On 3 March 1994, Nirvana's frontman, Kurt Cobain, checked into Room 541. At 6a.m. the following day, Cobain's wife, Courtney Love, found Kurt on the floor with blood trickling from one nostril and a suicide note in his left hand. Kurt survived this ghastly act of self-destruction only to then take his own life little over a month later, cementing his deification upon entry to the 27 Club (see page 50). Even if the hotel has been reticent with regards to Cobain's suicide attempt, they haven't tried to eradicate the episode by cutting the room in two (an act favoured by the Hotel Chelsea (see page 13) after the notorious Sid Vicious/Nancy Spungen incident) but neither, thankfully, have they named it the Kurt Cobain Room; that would have been far too crass and just not the Excelsior's style.

Those with a predilection for a minimalist approach should stay elsewhere, as the modus operandi here is to uphold a regal suaveness reminiscent of a grand Empire-style palace. And so it goes that, following a multimillion-euro renovation in 1999, the Excelsior's gilded decor appears as if airbrushed to perfection. Impressively, you don't need to book one of the more expensive premier suites to experience expansive accommodation; the guest rooms are roomy, with spacious bathrooms and 'heavenly beds' to ensure a good night's sleep, all within the most ornate of settings.

And herein lies the Excelsior's ethos: modern comforts modestly at hand amid the ostentatious shimmering chandeliers, faux chimneys and embellished furniture. Just one look up to the imposing facade rising unabashedly before you will tell you that this is a hotel for exhibitionists, braggarts or those simply feigning royal status. And there's nothing wrong with that; a reluctant rock star was even drawn to its charm.

The Westin Excelsior Hotel, Via Vittorio Veneto 125, Roma 00187, Italy

(+39) 06 47 081
excelsiorrome@westin.com
www.westinrome.com

SEE

ROME FILM FEAST
www.romacinemafest.it
Or to give it its full name: CINEMA Festa Internazionale di Roma. This film 'feast' is widely regarded as an important film festival and attracts movie-makers from all over the world. Taking place towards the end of the year – usually in October/November – it showcases the work of new directors and actors as well as honouring film legends such as Sean Connery and Meryl Streep.

FORTE PRENESTINO
Via Federico Delpino Centocelle, Roma 00171;
www.forteprenestino.net
An old fortress that has now become an entertainment area holding exhibitions and film screenings, and also hosting live music. In addition, it has a bookstore and, among other things, a body-piercing salon. So all your needs under one roof, then?

BE SEEN

BRANCALEONE
Via Levanna 13, Montesacro, Roma 00141; www.brancaleone.it
With an impressive programme of music, theatre and art, there is always something going on at the Brancaleone. Popular with locals, the music stage features rock, electronica and ska artists; Franz Ferdinand, Skream and The Skatalites have all played here.

L'OLIMPO

Hotel Bernini Bristol, Piazza Barberini 23, Roma 00187;
www.sinahotels.com

Mingle with the stars at this rooftop restaurant of the Hotel Bernini Bristol. With unsurpassed views across Rome, gourmet dining and an elite clientele, L'Olimpo's ornate decor and faultless service cannot fail to impress. This restaurant is also popular with royalty (Queen Elizabeth II has dropped in for dinner), so do dress smartly.

REST OF THE WORLD

COMPASS POINT

Picture this. Tropical turquoise waters lap against an empty stretch of white sand. The salubrious sea air has the palm trees nodding gently as they bask under the Bahamian sun. Rainbow-coloured huts promise tranquillity, far, as they are, from the holidaymakers holed up in the serried tourist traps.

It is, possibly, not the landscape you'd consider to be conducive to producing some of the world's most amped-up and rousing rock albums of all time, but many a rock 'n' roll deity has descended upon the island to lay down some tracks: David Bowie, U2, Judas Priest, The Cure and The Rolling Stones – all have been lured to the legendary Compass Point Studios. Maybe it's the awareness of how the distractions offered by the likes of London, Los Angeles and New York can impair a group's efficiency that encourages artists to step beyond the concrete city confines into the sealed world of serenity and creativity at Compass Point. Some of the most iconic musicians of all time have evidently felt drawn to the warm waters of Nassau. Iron Maiden returned for three consecutive albums and AC/DC recorded both 'Flick of the Switch' and the multimillion-selling 'Back in Black' here.

Both resort and studio were developed by Chris Blackwell, the music mogul who founded Island Records; though now, it is only the recording studio that is owned by the famous patriarch. Respected for his unique approach to the music business, Blackwell's famed modus operandi (his determination to support artistic endeavours regardless of mainstream appeal) appears to have extended to his other business interests too. His idiosyncratic style has left an indelible mark on Compass Point: the funky octagonal huts are an array of bold colours that jut out from a verdant bluff, as though a playground of children, hyper from too many E-numbers and armed with paintbrushes, had been unleashed upon the hillside. Though it's likely to be canoodling couples and the odd celebrity, and not kids, that you'll find emerging from these bright huts, squinting awkwardly into the Nassau sun.

The weathered-wood look of all the rooms might have you believing that the accommodation is as archaic and colonial as it is kooky. However, all the lodgings (compounds of huts, cottages and cabanas that run from the hills down to the sea) feature all the usual modern amenities while the rocking chairs and pine floors maintain a touch of Bahamian authenticity. All rooms have an ocean view and sit in close proximity to Love Beach – a two-mile stretch of private shoreline, ideal for a tranquil saunter once you've feasted on the cuisine and savoured the cocktails on the restaurant's open-air veranda.

Here, the only arduous task of the day, apart from snorkelling or kayaking, is deciding what to listen to – Grace Jones, Talking Heads, Ian Dury or Tom Tom Club, to name a few. So here's a tip to help you with that most onerous of tasks: 'Funky Nassau: The Compass Point Story' – a collection of various artists, ranging from reggae to post-punk, showcases some of the genre-defining music that has been created here, via the remixing skills of Compass Point's own famous producing stalwarts Sly & Robbie. Buy the album and you'll have the perfect soundtrack to your stay.

Come nightfall, Compass Point shakes off its sedate air and really wakes up. The restaurant and bar become loud and vibrant as locals and guests flock to the area for karaoke, which wails long into the night. On that note: cabana no. 113 is situated the furthest way from all the karaoke howling if it's not your bag. Of course, you could just dig deep and sing out a selection of your 'Island Classics', and don't be surprised if you find a celebrity trying his best at a Bob Marley track.

If you're in a band and want to capture some of Compass Point's magic in your own recordings, the studio asks you to get in touch, stating that they can help you with recording needs and 'coordinate your family holiday'. You can even take the dog. The studio (which actually sits next door to the resort) also has its own cabanas and cottages.

The last word, however, should go to Chris Blackwell, who oversaw the production of a huge ratio of great records at this serene location: 'you can make a record for anywhere your head imagines. Nassau's like a blank canvas'.

Compass Point Beach Resort, West Bay Street, PO Box CB 13842, Gambier, Nassau, Bahamas

(+1 242) 327 4500
reservations@compasspointbeachresort.com
www.compasspointbeachresort.com

SEE

JUNKANOO FESTIVAL
Nassau, Bahamas; www.junkanoo.com
A street parade with outlandish costumes and music, celebrated every Boxing Day and New Year's Day on the streets of Nassau. If you're not in Nassau over the festive period, then you can easily catch a glimpse of past Junkanoo celebrations in the sequences of various films – *Thunderball*, *After the Sunset* and *Jaws: The Revenge*.

FORT CHARLOTTE
West Bay Street, Nassau, Bahamas
If all the smiling tourists and sunshine starts to get to you, take a tour of Fort Charlotte and its dungeons. Built by the British in the

late 18th century to protect themselves against a US invasion, many of the original cannons are still in place. Intriguing exhibits and fantastic views.

BE SEEN

CLUB WATERLOO
Eastern Road, Nassau, Bahamas; www.clubwaterloo.com
This live music venue has something for all tastes – from rock to reggae. Things don't get going until late, mind, so turn up after 11p.m.

HAMMERHEADS BAR AND GRILL
East Bay Street, Nassau, Bahamas; www.hammerheadsnassau.com
Located between the two bridges to Paradise Island, Hammerheads is popular with locals, tourists, ex-pats and the yachting fraternity. Savour the relaxed atmosphere, pub-grub and happy-hour specials. Plus, check out local talent as the newest bands play Friday nights on the patio.

MARLEY RESORT

Just four miles from where his Island Records label boss and producer set up Compass Point Studios (see page 165), Bob Marley and his wife Rita discovered what they thought would make the ideal home from home. The problem was that, while the exterior of the perfect getaway exuded the promise of 'No More Trouble', those who owned the property were far from friendly. When the Marleys inquired as to its availability they were told: 'this house will never be sold to a black person'. Such an acerbic response proved a blow, not just because of the shamelessly racist nature of the remark but also because the Marleys really needed to seek respite from fame's spotlight, especially since Bob's high visibility as Rastafarian superstar had recently put him in the firing line.

Literally in the firing line: both Bob and Rita narrowly escaped assassination on 3 December 1976, days before a free concert in Kingston – Smile Jamaica. Both Marleys sustained injuries – but the incident, thankfully, didn't result in anyone's death. And, being the staunch advocate for peace that he was, Bob Marley took to the stage for Smile Jamaica just two days later, arm in a bandage, and let his honey-soaked voice do the fighting. Once again, Bob triumphed over adversity. Later, in 1982, it was Rita's turn to triumph after she purchased the home that she and Bob had previously received contemptuous warnings over.

After it had served as the Marleys' summer home for many years, the business-savvy Marley family decided to open its hand-carved doors to the world in 2007. Now, as Bob's music rings out from the resort's appropriately named Simmer Down restaurant, those walking the adjoining pillow-soft shore have their ears piqued by the sound of his skank guitar floating up into the cerulean sky. Poised on the edge of Cable Beach, this citrus-coloured reggae haven offers a unique glimpse into the irrepressible Marley legend: gold records sparkle from the wall, a gallery displays rare family photos and the Memorial Room features a rare biopic and concert footage while the listening stations play numerous interviews conducted with the revolutionary Rasta.

But this is no place at which to get all maudlin. Its sprightly rooms, named after Marley hits, are all prepped for chilling: the One Love Suite (for the honeymooning couple) offers a breathtaking oceanfront view, plus in-room whirlpool tub for two. The Royal Rita, where Rita Marley used to sleep, is decked out with mahogany flooring and furnishings and has the personal touch of featuring Mrs Marley's chaise longue. The Nice Time garden suite stands out by dislodging the regular bathroom layout, employed by the other standard suites, to make way for a whirlpool tub/shower to ensure you have more than just a nice time when bathing. In fact, all bathrooms seem to feature either a tropical rainfall shower or a whirlpool of some kind, making bath-time a great tension reliever. However, if you really want to unwind, head to the Natural Mystic Spa where 'Nana' Rita Marley's aromatherapy and herbal bath remedies will put you in the ultimate 'Mellow Mood'. But if you fear such languid living will leave you more placid than a cat, choose some activities to 'Lively Up Yourself' such as swimming with dolphins or scuba-diving.

The Stir It Up bar is the place to go for your rum and rhythm. Drop by on the right night and you could be listening to Stephen Marley jamming while you enjoy your Buffalo Soldier (the resort's own vodka cocktail). The rest of the spry Marley clan may also be found propping up the bar or in the Simmer Down restaurant cooking up a family recipe from a menu that features some of Bob's favourite cuisine. Another Marley sibling may be found in Marley's Boutique, an exclusive store that showcases Cedella Marley's Catch A Fire fashion designs.

The Marley Resort & Spa is not just a resort that has managed to lure you to an assemblage of Marley artefacts by way of rainbow-coloured charm; instead it's a place that pays genuine homage to Bob Marley, with the ever-present owners – the amiable Marley family – bringing the great man's peaceful vibe to the fore to ensure that your stay is a relaxing one. Very relaxing, as Bahamian clocks tend to tick more slowly than those in the rest of the world. In fact, you may find it very difficult to 'Lively Up Yourself' in the morning.

Marley Resort & Spa, West Bay Street, Cable Beach, Nassau, Bahamas

(+1 242) 702 2800
guestrelations@marleyresort.com
www.marleyresort.com

SEE

PARADISE ISLAND
www.nassauparadiseisland.com
Take a water taxi from Nassau's shore to this fantasy of an island, dreamed up by billionaire and philanthropist George Huntington Hartford II, for whom this was once a private home. Formerly called Hog Island, its world-famous Vegas-style casino, Atlantis, is a gambler's Utopia, reportedly paying out $35,000 every hour; it's a good place for celeb-spotting. Paradise Island has always attracted the stars: The Beatles' *Help!* movie was partially filmed here, as was the James Bond film *Thunderball*.

CORAL WORLD OCEAN PARK
6450 Estate Smith Bay, St Thomas, USVI 00802;
www.coralworldvi.com
Here you can marvel at the underwater world, without spoiling your hairdo or make-up, on one of the sea treks at Coral World Undersea Observatory. You just pop on a special helmet and take a stroll (Neil Armstrong style) on the seafloor, in its zero-gravity environment.

BE SEEN

SEÑOR FROG'S
West Bay Street, Nassau, Bahamas; www.senorfrogs.com
This popular restaurant and bar rakes in locals and tourists alike, encouraging them to let themselves go. The food won't set your tastebuds alight, but the atmosphere is positively searing. Not one for the timid: this place is loud.

FLUID LOUNGE AND CLUB
King's Court, Bay Street, Nassau, Bahamas
At the trendiest and newest club in town you won't go thirsty thanks to two full-service bars as well as a beer bar. Reserve a table in the VIP lounge upstairs for a more exclusive atmosphere.

COPACABANA PALACE

So, who do you think was first to trash a hotel, rock 'n' roll style? Led Zeppelin revving their Harleys in the halls of Chateau Marmont? A semi-naked Keith Moon driving a car into a pool before slipping on the remnants of his birthday cake at Flint's Holiday Inn? Or maybe it was Keith Richards, with his TV-hurling abilities?

Well, while all of the above made notable contributions to the imperial continuum of hotel-trashing, it was in fact Orson Welles who was credited with the first reported instance of rock 'n' roll defenestration. In 1942, Welles was staying at the Copacabana Palace when, freshly rebuffed by Dolores del Rio, he decided to take his anger out on the hotel furniture by launching it out of the window and into the pool below. What didn't make it into the pool was thrown about the room until security were able to restrain the fuming scriptwriter. Although, some claim that Welles' hotel-trashing fit was due to him being asked to complete his film *It's All True* on a minimal budget in Hollywood under the watchful gaze of Studio bosses, after Brazilian newspapers had made much of the controversy surrounding the film (a Brazilian fisherman – Welles had wanted the film to be as authentic as possible – was coerced into sailing treacherous waters for filming, and lost his life at sea: an accident blamed on Welles). Whatever the reason behind Orson's destructive rampage, it appears that all has been forgiven as Welles is just one of the hotel's past guests featured on a wall of captivating photographs that also includes the likes of Mick Jagger and Brazilian model Gisele Bündchen.

This legendary art-deco hotel remains as it did in Orson's day, with an air of exclusivity and original romance, while keeping apace with mod-con comfort. And with each spacious room in possession of the warm cream architectural angles that the hotel boasts on the outside, it is no wonder the five-star Copacabana Palace has continued to draw the celebrities and rock stars ever since Nat King Cole first lured the crowds to the hotel's Golden Room to hear his blend of baritone crooning and ivory tinkling.

Copacabana Palace, Avenida Atlântica 1702, Rio de Janeiro, CEP 22021 001, Brazil

(+55) 21 2548 7070
reservas@copacabanapalace.com.br
www.copacabanapalace.com

SEE

RIO CARNIVAL
Sambadrome, Rio de Janeiro; www.rio-carnival.net
If this festival has never shown up on your radar, here are a few essential need-to-knows: it starts 40 days before Easter and lasts four days; it is a party like no other; samba beats, huge decorative floats and extravagant dress fill the Sambadrome where the parade takes place. It also involves the whole of Rio, meaning the streets turn into full-blown party arenas too. The ball gowns are not donned by the street revellers but music and dancing prevails with the same, if not more, vigour and enthusiasm outside of the Sambadrome. What better way to immerse yourself in Brazilian culture?

PÃO DE AÇÚCAR (SUGAR LOAF MOUNTAIN)
Guanabara Bay, Rio de Janeiro
As the cable car trundles up to the peak of Sugar Loaf Mountain, eventually climbing high above the bustle of the city, you are treated to the most spectacular vista of Rio's opaque skyscrapers nestled between the dense forest and the mountains on one side and the fine lines of beach that border the ocean on the other. It's

only then that you'll appreciate the sheer size and scope of Brazil's second city. In the distance you should be able to see the outstretched arms of Cristo Redentor (Christ the Redeemer). Go at sunset (when there's less of a crowd, too) and you can't fail to find it breathtaking.

BE SEEN

CARIOCA DA GEMA
Rua Mem de Sá 79, Lapa, Rio de Janeiro;
www.barcariocadagema.com.br
Live music is an essential ingredient of Rio's nightlife and you won't have far to wander before stumbling across some; samba is the most popular. Carioca da Gema is famous – here you can dance any night of the week. With a casual dress code and a wide range of Brazilian snacks and drinks, this is the place to experience the chilled-out local culture.

CASA DA MATRIZ
Rua Henrique de Novaes 107, Botafogo, Rio de Janeiro;
beta.matrizonline.com.br
One of the few places in Rio where you can hear rock music, Casa da Matriz lies within a small house with two dancefloors and several bars and lounges, giving the place a house-party feel. Dance to a wide range of music including indie/pop rock, samba and reggae. A laidback atmosphere means those in Bermuda shorts and flip-flops won't be turned away.

ES SAADI

London, LA, New York... Yes, these are cities with obvious rock 'n' roll bolt-holes, but *Marrakesh*?

It is perhaps not the obvious choice for someone trailing rock 'n' roll's pale horse of destruction, and yet Morocco's 'red city' capital has welcomed the likes of Elton John and – if we're to stick with the apocalypse metaphor – the most venerated of rock music's pale riders, Led Zeppelin.

But it was the arrival of a tempestuous Rolling Stone that gave the Hotel Es Saadi its sordid affiliation with the foreboding presence of rock 'n' roll's shadowy side. Just one year before the Stones expressed sympathy for the devil and two before the cataclysmic Altamont Festival that signalled the end of the 60s utopian dream, the Stones had seemingly adopted a circus-like approach to living that evinced great tension and eventually disintegration among the group's internal relationships. And it would all come to a head at Hotel Es Saadi.

The group's blonde, raffish guitarist Brian Jones had managed to entice the other Stones and their assorted entourage to Morocco with news of a bohemian, hippy Mecca suffused with a Saharan charm of mythical proportions; a land where snake-charmers, acrobats and plenty of hashish would keep them entertained. The problem was that Jones, by this time, had become increasingly paranoid and violent as a result of substantial drug abuse, which only increased as the former band-leader was shunted out of the limelight by the formidable pairing of Mick Jagger and Keith Richards. Though, granted, Jones had reason to be suspicious of fellow guitar-slinger Richards as the 'elegantly wasted' Keef had been getting increasingly closer to Jones's girlfriend Anita Pallenberg (seemingly in direct proportion to the amount of abuse dished out to her by Jones) and Richards and Pallenberg were in the throes of their affair by the time they checked into the Es Saadi.

Despite Richards and Pallenberg disguising their affection by feigning nonchalance in each other's company, the ever-watchful Jones was suspicious of the couple and a palpable tension grew in the stupefyingly hot Moroccan air. The situation came to a head when Jones tried to coerce Pallenberg into an orgy with a couple of prostitutes at the hotel. When she resisted, Jones proceeded to throw food at her. Distressed at his vicious behaviour, Pallenberg fled from the scene in tears and made her way to Richards' room. Angry with Jones's humiliation of Anita, Richards resolved to rescue her from the constant torrent of abuse levelled at her from the unhinged Jones and so bundled his bruised beau into the back of a car and rock 'n' roll's new golden couple made their exit, leaving the rangy Mick Jagger to utter nasally from his plump lips 'it's gettin' fuckin' heavy...'

Allegedly, despite being roughed up at the hands of the maniacal Jones, Anita didn't want to leave the hotel. And it's easy to see why. For the egregious troupe, the opulent Hotel Es Saadi – bestowed as it is with distinct Moroccan architecture and regal ambience, sat within 8 hectares of lush tropical park with spectacular views of the snow-capped Atlas mountains – no doubt held considerable allure.

However, if the Stones entourage were billeted there today, the exotic pink-hued palace would hold even greater appeal given that the gilded hotel has since been augmented with 10 new villas, each one uniquely designed according to its own oriental theme. Shaded pathways weave their way through a labyrinth of colourful gardens flanking a hotel that echoes the traditionalism of the medina without losing any of its luxury and glamour. Nothing about this hotel is unassuming. Even the most discerning of deities will fail to pick out any fault with the hotel, including the service. Yet for all its grandeur, the Es Saadi also knows restraint; the decor never verges on the gaudy or tacky.

In summary, the hotel is one of contemporary comfort while never forgetting the beauty of its Moroccan heritage. You might be wondering when I'm going to harp on about how the rooms feature the latest gadgetry, with behemoth stereos and huge walk-in showers. Yes, all these elements are present, but the hotel has something else – something unique to its Moroccan roots. Something that no doubt even made the famously reserved and placid Rolling Stone drummer Charlie Watts break into song and dance.

Es Saadi Gardens and Resort, Rue Ibrahim El Mazini, Hivernage, Marrakesh 40000, Morocco

(+212) 5 24 44 88 11
info@essaadi.com
www.essaadi.com

SEE

NATIONAL FESTIVAL OF POPULAR ARTS
www.marrakechfestival.com
Middle of the year and the already teeming dusty streets are about to become a kiln as they overspill with people flocking to see the acrobats, snake-charmers, fire-eaters and a wealth of magicians, all conspiring to bring out the magic of Morocco's ancient past. Even the Al Badi Palace (remnants of a palace built by a 16th-century king) becomes a stage for the vibrant and traditional performances.

JAMAA EL FNA
Medina Quarter
Morocco not being a country renowned for its affiliation with rock 'n' roll, it's probably safe to say that there aren't too many rock 'n'

roll landmarks here. However, if you're a Robert Plant fan you may be only too aware of Plant's much anticipated reunion with former Zeppelin sidekick Jimmy Page for the Moroccan-influenced 'No Quarter' album in 1994. In conjunction with its release, Plant and Page recorded an *Unledded* performance for MTV – the footage for which was filmed in the Jamaa el Fna Square. If you're not on the Plant/Page trail, then head here anyway: the bustle of street-sellers and storytellers offers a glimpse into authentic Moroccan culture. It's also the best place to catch live music.

BE SEEN

LA MAMOUNIA HOTEL
Avenue Bab Jdid, Marrakesh 40040; www.mamounia.com
It may not be home to such a notoriously savage story of untamed rock stars as the Hotel Es Saadi, but it is certainly as breathtaking. And not without its rock 'n' roll credentials entirely, either. The Rolling Stones, Elton John and Led Zeppelin have all sauntered through the entry gardens and into the mosaic-tiled hotel where palatial furnishings fit for a king await unsuspecting guests. It also has the best bars.

KOSYBAR
47 Place des Ferblantiers, Marrakesh 40000; www.kosybar.com
Nightlife takes place out on the streets in Morocco, so rather than trying to match the ebullient mood outside, bar duties tend to include offering respite from the external mayhem. And the appropriately titled Kosybar does just that. With a roof terrace offering a superb vista over the medina, Kosybar proffers tourists and locals alike the chance to chill out with a cocktail while the sun sets over Marrakesh.

MANDARIN ORIENTAL
BANGKOK

Let's get something straight from the start: there are two types of rock star. Both are unnervingly cool; both can be marked out by their uncompromising regalia; both appear to have an edginess that would suggest their lives were borne from an exhilarating farrago of chaos and charisma that enables them to wring primal fun out of every minute of living. But one type is the pseudo-star, custom-designed to merely offer a charade of posed sneers and brooding looks for the cameras, and who can only muster the churlish behaviour of a child. The other type, while similar in appearance, possesses something more than just 'surface cool' and invokes the very spirit of rock 'n' roll by truly existing on the wild side.

Billy Idol is the real deal in rock-star terms. After a short tenure fronting Generation X, the punk-rock vocalist went solo, became an MTV staple and, by the mid 1980s, found himself in the vice-like grip of some dangerous dependencies. By 1989, following the split from long-time girlfriend Perri Lister who had tired of his insatiable appetite for destruction, Idol decided a break in Thailand was needed. But this was not to be a trip to free himself of the engulfing excesses that had left him estranged from Perri. Oh no.

Checking into a sumptuous suite at the Mandarin Oriental – an imposing regal hotel perched on the banks of the Chao Phraya River – Idol cooked up a maelstrom of debauchery with an assembly of prostitutes. Stuffed to the gills with drugs, the sneering rocker's sense of feng shui had obviously been obliterated as he set about defiling the extravagance of his perfectly appointed room by demolishing furniture, reducing his TV to rubble and spilling all manner of liquids on the carpets.

But this was far from being the end of Idol's Thai blowout. Although, it has to be said, details are sketchy. Newspaper reports claim Idol went on to two further hotels – The Royal Cliff (out on the coast) and Bangkok's Royal Orchid Sheraton – to continue his orgy of hard-drinking, hotel-trashing and drug-taking, and racked up an enormous bill (its equivalent for this spiky-haired libertine could have been a lifetime's supply of peroxide). Other reports state that Idol ended his three-week binge at the Oriental after having been shot with tranquilliser darts by the Thai army, after refusing to leave his suite. (The Hard Rock Hotel Penang in Malaysia even went on to pay homage to Idol's Thai wrecking-spree by encasing the stretcher that carried Idol out of the Oriental in glass and placing it on the wall.)

Incredulously, this drug-induced altercation with the Thai army was not to be the *coup de grâce* for Idol's hard-living and boorish ways. Subsequent years would see the bovine Billy nearly lose his leg in a motorcycle accident, go to court for punching a woman in the face and then very nearly die in a drug overdose. If only Billy had taken a moment to enjoy some of the finer things in life, he may have been able to palliate some of his destructive urges; what's more, the Mandarin Oriental is the perfect place to try such things.

The Oriental's meticulous approach to service (every guest has access to a personal butler), the traditional Thai spa, classes in yoga and t'ai ch'i, and the winsome notes quoting famous authors that are left on guests' pillows – reminding them of the wonders of sleep – could surely sweeten the most sardonic of sneers. And the hotel's tranquil touches don't end there: there's also the colonial charm of the Author's Lounge, which comes complete with white wicker chairs and homemade scones. But if such sedateness had been to the singer's chagrin, he could have easily opted for something more invigorating – lessons in Thai cooking or a Thai Culture course.

If you're finding such activities as unpalatable as the image of a leather-clad rocker, visibly glutted with drugs, serving up your dim sum, fear not – you could always retire to the jungle setting of Bamboo Bar for an Oriental Mai Tai. But before you try to up the ante to Billy Idol levels, remember that Thailand has strict laws when it comes to drugs. Billy was lucky to only get a dart in the backside... So, on that note, how does a spot of afternoon tea in the Author's Lounge sound?

Mandarin Oriental, 48 Oriental Avenue, Bangkok 10500, Thailand

(+66) 2 659 9000
mobkk-enquiry@mohg.com
www.mandarinoriental.com/bangkok

SEE

THE VEGETARIAN FESTIVAL
Phuket; www.phuketvegetarian.com
Not so much a festival that supports vegetarianism as a celebration of abstinence. After six days of going without alcohol, sex and meat (hence the name) those partaking in the festivities are said to become bewitched by spirits. Then, to prove their bodies exist in a truly spiritual realm free of physical constraints, they walk on hot coals and pierce body parts with swords, skewers and fishing rods. And if you need a visual distraction from all that piercing, then there is an awesome firework display.

PATTAYA INTERNATIONAL MUSIC FESTIVAL
Pattaya; www.pattayamusicfest.com
This three-day music festival takes place every March on Pattaya Beach with both home-grown and international acts performing.

Making room for a variety of genres, this festival – Thailand's biggest – attracts throngs of locals and tourists alike.

BE SEEN

RCA – ROYAL CITY AVENUE
Bangkok
Although the Royal City Avenue (or RCA, as it's known) is one of the biggest and busiest entertainment areas, it's also one of the least-known to visitors. With a multitude of bars, clubs and restaurants, it has something for everyone. While you're here, check out two of the best non-expat clubs – Slim and Route 66.

THE ROCK PUB
Hollywood Street Building, Radchatewee, Payathai Road, Bangkok; www.therockpub-bangkok.com
Diehard fans of 80s and 90s metal should make a beeline to The Rock Pub. This must-visit live music venue has hosted gigs by Halogen, DragonForce, Doro and Exodus in its 20-year history.

SOFITEL BRISBANE

Everyone's favourite Brummie, Ozzy Osbourne, shuffled into the Sofitel Brisbane when he landed in the Sunshine State with his wife-cum-manager Sharon. Now, you may be thinking: the 'Blizzard of Ozz' swoops down on Oz and leaves behind him a trail of massacred menageries, an army of ants doused in urine and a dry bar. But to recite such tales would be too glib and obvious, and those stories have been told more times than Ozzy has stammered an expletive. The only animal Ozzy put inside his mouth during his stay was chicken, and he had it served up just like everybody else in the hotel: plucked, cooked and with gravy; which, incidentally, must have suited his palate as he reportedly ordered it twice.

Sure, Ozzy may no longer be the *enfant terrible* of rock 'n' roll, but this five-star luxury hotel certainly seems capable of quelling any modicum of rock-star behaviour. From the moment you step inside the glistening lobby that exudes courtly elegance but without the stuffiness, a feeling of refined glamour embraces you. A sense of buoyant calm exists throughout; to personify the hotel would be to deem it as composed but not repressed, excitable yet also unflappable. It is probably this aura of laidback confidence (aided by jovial staff) that enabled an energetic Robbie Williams to treat guests to an impromptu performance in the piano lounge without causing too much hysteria. The same sense of benevolence and relaxed blitheness obviously also touched Californian pop-rockers Maroon 5, as they dished out free concert tickets to hotel guests during their stay here, again, without a frenzied guest in sight.

Those with the remotest interest in ephemeral reality-TV celebrities who create the luminous headlines on a glut of gossip

mags may know that famous socialite Nicole Richie hooked up
with Good Charlotte vocalist Joel Madden here and retired
from the type of maddening scenes often enjoyed by
celebutantes. Taking a sabbatical from such furore, Nicole could
be seen to be back on an even keel and getting a pedicure at the
hotel's Spa Retreat, while hubby Joel, taking a break from a
world tour, also joined her to enjoy the ethereal qualities of the
spa before the two were spotted canoodling, blissfully unaware
of the world around them.

By now, you may have conjured up an image in your head
that sails pretty close to the setting of an ultra-romantic retreat,
where the soft murmur of the languid is broken only by the
chirping of incorrigible romantics. So, where are the scabrous
tales? Where is the party? Where is the raucous roar of rock
stars trapped in the realms of believing their own hype? Well,
this is the pristine sanctuary to which rock stars retire in order
to tune in and drop out – in the meditative sense, not the
intoxicated one. However, requirements for the rock-star doyens
have not been forsaken. The palatial Opera Suite, for example, is
split over two floors, bathed in natural light and has been
bestowed with every convenience for the moneyed guest: spa
bath, double showerheads, walk-in wardrobe, a sizeable
workspace, a swirling staircase to lead you up to your sumptuous
lounge and enticing bedroom, along with a private kitchen.
When Kylie Minogue stayed she brought along her own chef to
make the most of the kitchen facilities. Not that you should feel
the need to bring any culinary help because the Thyme^2
restaurant offers up an array of delicious seafood; though the
oysters may well see you excitedly making your way back to the
soft linen of your bed with a loved one.

Luxury abounds across the plush suites and deluxe lounges
in Club Sofitel. This exclusive club, up on the 30th floor, affords
the VIP treatment together with knockout views across the city.

In one of these rooms you'll get to experience the inspired design of the MyBed, which will leave you believing you have never truly slept before. If that's not enough, the relaxation factor can take you higher into the ether with the top-floor swimming pool, so why not take a midnight dip high in the Brisbane sky? Oh, and remember, the chicken comes highly recommended.

Sofitel Brisbane Central, 249 Turbot Street, Brisbane, QLD 4000, Australia

(+61) 07 3835 3535
h5992@accor.com
www.sofitelbrisbane.com.au

SEE

BIG DAY OUT FESTIVAL
Gold Coast; www.bigdayout.com
Australia's biggest music festival, attracting the biggest international names, takes place across several cities in January/February; Metallica, Muse, Nirvana and The Prodigy are just a few of the headliners to have taken to the stage. Although the festival doesn't actually hit Brisbane, it's only about an hour's drive away, on the Gold Coast (which isn't that far if you consider the vastness of this country). If you're not driving, getting to the Gold Coast is still fairly easy: buses from the Roma Street Transit Centre run to the Gold Coast about eight times a day.

RIVERWALK
Even rock gods need a helping hand to walk on water, which is where this half-a-mile floating walkway comes in handy. Be at one with the river as the walkway rises and falls with the tide. Should you wish to carry on, the floating walkway connects over many walks along the Brisbane River.

BE SEEN

THE ZOO
711 Ann Street, Fortitude Valley, QLD 4006; www.thezoo.com.au
Nope, not the place where animals are kept in cages, but a versatile music venue that has been pivotal in helping Brisbane gain recognition as a viable breeding ground for new music (*Billboard* magazine voted the city as one of the Top 5 International Music Hotspots). What started as a café and pool hall at the tail end of 1992 soon became the hub from which a wealth of new independent music emerged. With live music ranging from rock to folk to reggae, this long-standing venue has proved that this laidback city has a thriving live music scene. It is one of the best clubs in Brisbane.

RIC'S CAFÉ AND BAR
321 Brunswick Street, Fortitude Valley, QLD 4006; www.ricsbar.com.au
The place to hear new up-and-coming bands, Ric's Bar initially appears too small even to have a stage. If you don't hear the Next Big Thing in the indie scene, however, you'll at least be treated to some diverse and original sounds. You can even get a nice greasy breakfast here after a hard night out.

BIBLIOGRAPHY

The following books have proved to be invaluable references:

Harris, John: *Hail! Hail! Rock 'n' Roll: The Ultimate Guide to the Music, the Myths and the Madness* (Sphere, 2009)

Moynihan, Michael; Søderlind, Didrik: *Lords of Chaos: The Bloody Rise of the Satanic Metal Underground* (Feral House, 1998)

Hoskyns, Barney: *Hotel California: Singer-songwriters and Cocaine Cowboys in the LA Canyons 1967–1976* (Fourth Estate, 2005)

Kent, Nick: *The Dark Stuff: Selected Writings on Rock Music 1972–1993* (Faber & Faber, 2007)

Davis, Stephen: *Hammer of the Gods: Definitive Biography of Led Zeppelin* (Pan Books, 1995)

Sixx, Nikki: *The Heroin Diaries: A Year in the Life of a Shattered Rock Star* (Simon & Schuster, 2007)

Cross, Charles R: *Heavier than Heaven: The Biography of Kurt Cobain* (Hodder & Stoughton, 2001)

Index

Index

Index

ACKNOWLEDGEMENTS

Rock 'n' Roll Hotels
Researched and written by: Greg Simmons
Publisher: Jonathan Knight
Editors: Nikki Sims, Sophie Dawson
Cover Design and Illustrations: Harriet Yeomans
Proofreader: Leanne Bryan
PR: Shelley Bowdler
Published by: Punk Publishing, 3 The Yard, Pegasus Place,
London SE11 5SD
Distributed by: Portfolio Books, 2nd Floor, Westminster House,
Kew Road, Richmond TW9 2ND

The publishers and author have done their best to ensure the
accuracy of all information in *Rock 'n' Roll Hotels*, however, they
can accept no responsibility for any injury, loss or inconvenience
sustained by anyone as a result of information contained in this
book.

Punk Publishing takes its environmental responsibilities
seriously. This book has been printed on paper made from
renewable sources and we continue to work with our printers to
reduce our overall environmental impact.

Greg Simmons would like to thank:
Jonathan Knight, Sophie Dawson and everyone at Punk
Publishing; editor Nikki Sims; Kim Okeson at Andaz West
Hollywood; Nic Adler at the Roxy; Mick Wall for his George
V/Black Sabbath story; Rhys Herdman for casting his keen eye
over initial drafts; Victoria Pearson (*tiny thumbs up!*); Stuart

Catley; Kevin Nickells; Andy Neary; my bro Jon Paul. Hello to all my Bristol Peeps (I miss you) and Brummie cohorts. Special thanks to my parents, who continue to support and encourage my creative endeavours. No matter how crazy.